ACCESS ALL
AREAS

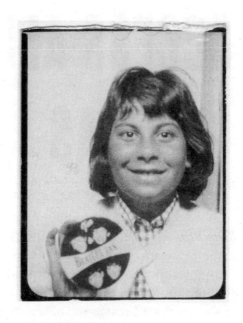

About the Author

Born in Chicago, Barbara moved to London after graduating from Northwestern University. The first half of her career was spent as a music journalist working for *NME*, *Sounds*, *Rolling Stone*, *Crawdaddy* and *Cream* before writing the authorised biography *Keith Richards: Life As A Rolling Stone* in 1979.

In November 2000, after almost twenty years at Warner Brothers, Barbara co-founded leading independent music agency MBCPR with Moira Bellas where she still works now. Within six months it became one of the country's top music PR firms. The current client roster includes: Madonna, Mark Ronson, Foo Fighters, Elvis Costello, Keith Richards, Rod Stewart, Kasabian, Metallica, Depeche Mode, Texas, Rag'n'Bone Man, St Vincent, Pearl Jam, Olly Murs, Ray Davies and Rufus Wainwright.

In November 2001, Charone and her business partner, Moira Bellas, were honoured as Women of the Year by Nordoff-Robbins Music Therapy and The Brit Trust. Then, in both 2006 and 2009, Barbara won the coveted Music Week Press Award. Last summer she became a Board Director of Chelsea Football Club.

First published in Great Britain in 2022 by White Rabbit
This paperback edition first published in Great Britain in 2023
by White Rabbit,
an imprint of The Orion Publishing Group Ltd
Carmelite House, 50 Victoria Embankment
London EC4Y 0DZ

An Hachette UK Company

1 3 5 7 9 10 8 6 4 2

A CIP catalogue record for this book
is available from the British Library.

ISBN (Mass Market Paperback) 978 1 4746 2227 1
ISBN eBook 9781474622288
ISBN Audio 9781474622295

Typeset by Input Data Services Ltd, Somerset

Printed and bound in Great Britain by Clays Ltd, Elcograf S.p.A.

MIX
Paper from
responsible sources
FSC
www.fsc.org   FSC® C104740

www.whiterabbitbooks.co.uk
www.orionbooks.co.uk

ACCESS ALL AREAS

A Backstage Pass Through
50 Years of Music and Culture

Barbara Charone

WHITE
RABBIT

Contents

Foreword by Elvis Costello   vii
Prologue: London Calling   ix

1   Born in the USA   1
2   I'm On the Guest List!   17
3   It's Only Rock 'n' Roll   29
4   Sing Me Back Home   49
5   All That Jazz   61
6   Lucky Star   73
7   Crazy for You   87
8   Constant Craving   101
9   True Blue   113
10   Independence Day   125
11   Oh What a World   141
12   Somewhere Over the Rainbow   149
13   Comedy Central   167
14   Band Aid   181

My Phone's On Vibrate for You . . .   197

Foreword

'Barbara Through the Looking Glass'

I've known the name of 'Barbara Charone' on an inky byline only a little longer than we have been friends, but it was not until reading from this immensely entertaining and engaging memoir that I realised how much our stealthy approach to the music world resembled a funhouse reflection.

BC arrived in London in 1973, the same year that I went up to London to meet the Queen, my belongings wrapped in a handkerchief on a stick and a cat under my arm. Well, not quite, but I had moved from Liverpool to seek my fortune and found a world to be much as Barbara describes it when she arrived in England from Chicago.

In the few short years prior to landing in London, it seems we shared an enthusiasm for musical artists about which our classmates had little curiosity. During those parallel years, BC returned frequently to her hometown of Chicago to catch exciting shows, from a musically barren university town in Missouri, while I skipped school to see some of the very same artists in Manchester, a mere forty miles from my home in Liverpool. Okay, I didn't have a supercool orange Austin Mini Metro, but I had a return train ticket and a stout pair for boots for standing in festival mud.

The world that you'll find in these pages will be familiar if you lived through those days, or you are only looking back at them; the television shows we watched, the jokes we shared, the songs to which we shuffled and danced or suffered heartbreak are almost the same, only with a little time difference or a slight jet lag involved. So are the reputations at which we scoffed, the legends we burnished with our dreams and praise.

Records that didn't hit the hit parade were sometimes fly-bys, other times delicious, shared secrets and precious obscurities, whispers and mere rumours of greatness. Someone has to tell these tales. I tried to do it in song and BC has done it as both a journalist and a publicist but also as a confidante, a friend and even as a rival, if misguided, football fan of her beloved Chelsea.

BC's unmistakable voice is caught here, like her laughter, honesty, loyalty and relentless love for life and music, and all that makes me thankful for her tugging my sleeve from time to time when she knew it might be better for me to walk away from a scrap – or attend to her voice teasing and reasoning that I should let myself go and jump right in to some new encounter or scheme.

For all that you will find within, this is the work you can do and fun that you can have with a true pal.

And as I like to remind Barbara, 'You'll Never Walk Alone'.

Elvis Costello, Liverpool, 26 November 2021

Prologue: London Calling

It promised to be a weekend like no other. It was a lovely warm day in June 1974. Paul McCartney and Wings had the number 1 single with 'Band on the Run'. Crowds flocked to see Paul Newman and Robert Redford in *The Sting. Happy Days* had America enthralled as the Fonz ruled in his first season on TV. Nixon was still president, though only just. And I was finally graduating university. Soon school would be out, not just for summer but forever.

After four years and three different universities, I was finally graduating with a BA in English from Northwestern University, a prestigious 'Big Ten' school outside Chicago. I was headed to the football stadium where the ceremony would take place. It was a beautiful summer day, just ripe for a celebration.

I'd minored in creative writing, having done my senior-year thesis on Raymond Chandler. I was a massive fan of his infamous detective Philip Marlowe and for my final paper attempted to write a short story in his inimitable style. I had fun with the film-noir genre, and my story, 'Summer Snow', about a drug deal gone wrong, earned me top marks and helped me graduate with honours.

I left my parents' house in Glencoe, a snug middle-class suburb not too far from Lake Michigan on a street dotted with more than a few original Frank Lloyd Wright houses. I'd been living at home since returning from London just before the start of my senior year in the autumn of 1973. It took about twenty minutes to drive to the graduation ceremony along Lake Michigan. My parents, lawyer dad and freelance drama teacher mom, would meet me there after the ceremony. I drove with the mandatory graduation cap on the seat of my orange Austin Mini Metro and the graduation gown rolled up to my knees, music blasting on the 8-track player, windows wide open to let the smoke from the proverbial joint waft away into the lovely summer air.

The car was my pride and joy, and not just because it was so easy to spot in parking lots after attending concerts when stoned. It must have been the only orange Austin Mini Metro in the whole of Illinois. My parents gave it to me when I graduated high school four years earlier in 1970. The car mirrored my obsession with all things British. It reminded me of a youth spent watching *A Hard Day's Night*, *Help*, even *Having a Wild Weekend* (Dave Clark Five, but don't judge), James Bond films, *The Man From U.N.C.L.E.* (I loved David McCallum) and of course all those albums by the Rolling Stones, the Beatles, the Kinks, the Who and countless others. Now, as I drove along the leafy streets, my thoughts were squarely focused on the future. And what a future lay ahead of me. I was moving to London at the end of the summer to take a full-time job with one of the four weekly music papers that existed then, called *Sounds*. Not surprisingly, I could not wait.

My time at university was quite an adventure in itself. I'd started out at the University of Missouri in Columbia because they had a top journalism school and I saw my future as a writer. Despite the quality of the classes, I wasn't really happy living in Columbia. After growing up in the Chicago area, with all it had to offer on my doorstep, it was hard to accept their small-town mentality and lack of big-city pursuits. It seemed like my classmates were all two years behind what I and my friends had done in high school: music, books, films, politics, drugs – the whole nine yards.

As the University of Missouri was a Big Ten school, much of campus life was dominated by the football team and our dorm was deserted when they played at home. We used to ride our bikes round the deserted hallways on those Saturdays. I don't know why I didn't go to the games as I love sports, but I suppose the eighteen-year-old rebel in me looked down on the culture of college football.

The place I gravitated to in the small town was the local record store where I religiously bought *Rolling Stone* magazine every fortnight, followed by most of the albums that sounded good from their incredible review section. They also had occasional in-store visits from bands playing on campus – not quite *Spinal Tap* but close. The highlight of my first year was when the Byrds came to town.

If you wanted to see a major band or artist you had to go to either Kansas City or neighbouring St Louis, and neither lived up to the sophisticated delights of the Windy City. And quite honestly there was no one, really, to go with. My classmates were mostly provincial and had never heard of half the bands I loved. I couldn't get anyone interested in seeing Rod Stewart and the Faces because they'd never heard of them. Or Neil Young. Or any other favourites back in the autumn of 1970.

So I went to Chicago at least once a month, ostensibly to visit my parents because they were paying for the short sixty-minute flight, but the real reason was to see Joni Mitchell or Jackson Browne or The Band or the Doors. Music dominated most of my waking hours. When I stayed in Columbia,

I mostly hung with a girl from Ohio whose boyfriend had given her a big bag of pills to sell for pocket money but quite often, as we'd sit eating in the dreary cafeteria, not having any plans for the evening or weekend ahead, we found ourselves dipping into that bag.

There was no way I would last four years in Missouri without losing my sanity, so for my sophomore year I transferred back to Chicago, to Northwestern University (an even better school which ironically also had a Big Ten football team), and lived in a dorm on campus. I drove my beloved orange Mini Metro to the city for shows all the time. And I drove home frequently to have my mom do my washing and get some home-cooked meals.

Northwestern was fantastic. The classes were challenging and the campus, which was right on Lake Michigan, was absolutely beautiful though it was hard to get out of bed in the winter for class when the temperature – driven by that famous Chicago wind – was well below zero. It was a bit easier to get out of bed for the fairly frequent anti-Vietnam War demonstrations (1971–72). Feelings against Nixon and the futility of the war raged within most of us, driven by the sentiments expressed in the music of many of the artists we loved.

It was at one of those shows in the city that I accosted the music critic for the *Chicago Sun Times*, Al Rudis, and told him what I wanted to do what he did when I grew up. I'd been writing frequently for my high school paper and, having grown up in a house full of books, daily Chicago papers, the *New York Times* and the influential *New Yorker* magazine, I was an avid reader.

Al was very approachable. Sensing my enthusiasm for rock journalism knew no bounds, he suggested I send him a couple of ideas for articles. The first thing I wrote was an

6

opinion piece about James Taylor. His sudden rise to fame had captivated America (he'd been on the cover of *Time* magazine), along with his personal life and his song 'Fire and Rain' about a friend's suicide. The story was accepted, much to my surprise and delight. I'll never forget the excitement when I picked up a copy of the paper at the local drugstore and raced through the pages till I found the story and saw my byline. From that point on I was hooked and on track for a career in journalism, music and adventure.

By the time I landed in London on the Tufts University programme in September 1972 I had a few articles under my belt and the enthusiasm of youth racing through my veins. The students were housed in a bed and breakfast on Stanhope Gardens in South Kensington, and I showed my ability to talk my way into almost anything (obviously a PR career beckoned) by getting the only single room in the place on the grounds that it would be unfair of me to share, as I would be constantly coming in late from my rock 'n' roll travels and waking my roommate. Always considerate.

The nice man at the *Chicago Sun Times* had offered to run any interesting interviews, especially on British artists who were playing shows in Chicago, so the incentive was there and I was determined to take full advantage of the opportunity. It didn't take long to make friends, one of whom worked in the press office at a major record company, WEA. That woman was Moira Bellas and she remains one of my best friends. We've worked together for the past forty years, eventually at the record label and for over two decades with our own PR company, MBC. But I'm getting way ahead of the story.

It was an incredible year and a really unusual programme. We had a history class at the Victoria and Albert museum. The film critic from the weekly listings magazine *Time Out* taught creative writing. We often clashed as I was slightly arrogant – blame it on youth – because my articles were already being published. I suppose I was what you'd call 'a know-it-all'.

London was exciting and exotic despite the fact that there were only three TV channels, no central heating, no reports in the papers of American sports (not even the scores) and the best hamburger on offer was a Wimpy. The pizza was not even worth a mention.

Through my contacts I got invited to some tapings of the legendary BBC music programme, *The Old Grey Whistle Test*, where bands played live. I quickly became a regular at record company press receptions, of which there were many.

I met other rock writers and, after much persistence and even more phone calls, finally got *NME* (*New Musical Express*) to agree to let me write for them. At the time *NME* was *the* music paper (there were four if you counted *Record Mirror*, but it was far superior to *Melody Maker* and *Sounds*), led by influential writers like Nick Kent and Charles Shaar Murray, so I was in good company and hungry to learn.

When the university programme finished in June, I moved into a flat off Finchley Road, writing for the *NME*, mostly stuff no one else wanted to cover like Grateful Dead wannabes Hawkwind on a bank holiday weekend or synth rock auteurs Genesis. Those *NME* boys didn't like prog rock one bit. I also continued to publish regularly in the *Chicago Sun Times*, so life was sweet. My big breakthrough came just before I left when by chance I stumbled upon the Who recording what was to become *Quadrophenia* in their studio in Battersea. How I got in, God knows, but I had a genuine scoop, and *NME* were impressed with my bravado.

On the day before I was due to start my senior year at Northwestern, I flew back to Chicago, clearing customs with a lump of hash in my pocket and a sign above my head that read: 'Keep America Drugs Free'. Much to my parents' relief I made it back in time.

Senior year flew by. I was back living with my parents after my London adventure and now a US correspondent for *NME*, sending features and live reviews to London. Lucky for me, Bob Dylan reunited with the Band and their world tour started in Chicago in January 1974, so *NME* went big on that, along with later interviews and live reviews: Joni Mitchell, Linda Ronstadt, Roger McGuinn (the Byrds). A big CSN&Y (Crosby, Stills, Nash & Young) tour hit Chicago too, and my old friends Genesis played a show.

I'd also started writing for the *Chicago Reader*, an excellent free weekly indie paper that covered a lot of music. I was building up quite a portfolio and, fuelled with ambition, I began ringing *Rolling Stone* – actually haranguing them, bombarding them with ideas, not taking no for an answer. Once again that innate ability to persuade helped me get my first assignment, a live review of a James Taylor and Carly Simon concert in Milwaukee, Wisconsin (an hour from Chicago). Funny how James Taylor got me my first printed piece in a major city paper and later my first published piece in the music bible *Rolling Stone*.

Later that summer I landed my first feature assignment for *Rolling Stone*, a story on the band War, no longer with their lead singer Eric Burden. They were playing in Detroit, which unlike Chicago had no downtown centre, and having lost the record company contact at the show, I had no way back to the hotel and found myself one of the only white kids outside the venue. It seemed like an eternity before a taxi driver miraculously appeared.

The experience reminded me of when I was sixteen and, having just got my driving licence, drove my parents' Buick (a rather big, flash car) down to the south side of Chicago with a bunch of girlfriends to witness first hand a real Chicago blues club, with a makeshift stage only a foot off the ground. The music was incredible, but when four sixteen-year-old white kids from the suburbs walked in the door, heads turned.

Back in 1970, even in a metropolitan city like Chicago, there was definitely a sense of segregation pervading the live music scene. We were all oblivious to the rules of past generations and keen on moving forward together. We embraced so much of what was then referred to as black music. It was only when you actually went to a show that you realised you stood out as a minority.

By then I was also writing for *Creem* magazine, an upstart publication based in Detroit and the home of Lester Bangs, one of the original gonzo rock critics. An obsessive Who fan, I once interviewed Toots and the Maytals while they were supporting the Who for a story in *Creem*. Being a stranger to the quality of Jamaican pot, I foolishly ignored all warnings from friends and smoked with Toots during the interview. All I could understand him saying within a few puffs was: 'Praise the Lord! Praise the Lord!' Afterwards I sat, shell shocked in my rental car in the Holiday Inn car park, unable to drive and wondering how the hell I was going to write a 2500-word feature on what I'd just experienced!

Years later when the Rolling Stones' label signed Peter Tosh and Mick Jagger duetted with him on the wonderful single 'You Gotta Walk and Don't Look Back', I wised up and declined Peter's offer of a spliff in the Kingston, Jamaica Sheraton, when we did an interview. However, he was kind enough to leave the rest of the joint, which resembled a small tree, with me for the remainder of my stay.

Soon summer was over and I was finally heading back

to London, to take up full-time employment as a rock critic on an established weekly British music paper. While *Rolling Stone* was pre-eminent in the US, London was really where it was at in the autumn of 1974. Where America had both coasts and everything in between, the UK music scene pretty much *was* London, so it was an incredibly exciting place to live.

Female rock critics were extremely rare back then. There was a lot of stereotyped clichés surrounding women writers. I remember the first time I went backstage at Madison Square Garden, in New York City, for a Who show, the security guard on the door laughed in my face when I said I was on the guest list, dismissing me with a sarcastic: 'Yeah, sure you are.' I had to repeat my name several times and insist he look again at the list. It was straight out of that iconic film *Almost Famous*. The security guards just looked at you as if you were what they referred to as groupie. They couldn't understand why a woman would come backstage for any other reason.

Rock critics were almost eclusively male and the only women I could remember on the *NME* were the editor's secretary and a female photographer from New York City. I was incredibly lucky to get the job on *Sounds*. A vacancy existed only because the respected writer Penny Valentine had just quit and they obviously wanted another woman to replace her.

It was most definitely a man's world and continued to be so throughout the seventies and well into the eighties. Not just on newspapers and magazines but in record companies too. Women were mostly relegated to PA or secretarial roles and occasionally travel or artist relations (the people who sorted out the parties) or press. Serious jobs like writers, editors or managing directors were almost exclusively male.

An old boyfriend from junior high was studying at the

London School of Economics and had a spare room in a flat on Sloane Street, in Chelsea, opposite Cadogan Gardens. It was a great area, just off the the King's Road, which I knew from all those movies about London in the sixties. I eagerly moved in and began the commute from Sloane Square tube to Holloway Road, Islington where *Sounds* was based on Benwell Road (not far from Arsenal's old Highbury ground).

By an astonishing quirk of fate, my first big assignment for *Sounds* was to interview Keith Richards and Mick Taylor for a massive seven-page (those were the days) special on the Rolling Stones to coincide with the release of their seminal *It's Only Rock 'n' Roll* album. I was obsessed with the Stones from a young age. Having bought their early albums and then eagerly waiting for a new one to come out, my parents at one point told me: 'Enough is enough. Why do you need another one?' They just didn't get it.

My father later developed a liking for the band, so much so that I took him to see the weirdest show I've ever been to when the band toured *Exile on Main Street* in 1972. Due to overwhelming demand, they scheduled a matinee show at 4 p.m. You can only imagine the state of the band when they ambled onstage, most likely not having been to bed. But what went on behind closed doors was something I could only speculate about back then. All that was about to change.

So it was with some trepidation and an awful lot of excitement that I made my way to the Atlantic Records offices on Berners Street, just off Oxford Street, for my interviews. Prior to this I had clung to the belief that the Rolling Stones were all about Mick Jagger, one of the best front men to ever grace a stage or front a band.

The room I was ushered into was decorated like a hotel room, Keith style, with scarves draped over the lamps, dim lights, candles and incense burning. The scene was set, the door opened and Keith Richards walked in. I later wrote: 'When Keith Richards walks in a room, rock 'n' roll walks in after him.' From that point onwards, my whole perception of the Rolling Stones and modern music took a seismic shift. He didn't so much move as sway. He didn't so much talk as rhythmically strut. I was hooked. I was twenty-two years old and life would never be the same.

At home, Glencoe, Illinois, late 60s

Chapter 1
Born in the USA

I was eleven years old when the Beatles invaded America. And I was fully prepared. The first single I remember buying was 'Mack the Knife' by Bobby Darin. I'd grown up in a house full of Frank Sinatra and Ella Fitzgerald so this tune was a natural extension of that era. Ditto 'Moon River' by Andy Williams. It didn't take me long however to discover the guitar, and just before the Beatles swooped, I had been a big fan of records like 'Louie Louie' by the Kingsmen, a rock 'n' roll classic.

I was in the sixth grade at North School in Glencoe. We had just moved into the house I would live in till I went to university. My earliest school memories are of frequently being sent to the hall for talking in class. One year my teacher moved my desk next to hers on the second day of class so she could keep an eye on me, and it was not unusual for report cards to say: 'Barbara tends to monopolise discussion at all times' – good experience for a future writer. Once my younger sister started school, I lived in fear she would see me out in the hall (a bit like detention, you sat at a desk in the hall outside the classroom on your own) and tell our parents.

The house was a lovely old English-style Tudor home, not far from Lake Michigan where we spent much of our summer vacations at the beach. Lake Michigan is one of the five Great Lakes in the Midwest, and to call it a lake really does this massive expanse of water an injustice. It's more akin to what Europeans would call a sea. It was that big.

In the winter we'd ice-skate on one of several local ponds and build snowmen in our nicely sized garden. The house was built on a ravine. You had to drive over a small historic Frank Lloyd Wright bridge to get to it. It was absolutely picturesque.

We moved there in the summer of 1963. I now had my own room and, even better, my own bathroom, which came in handy as I listened to the top 40 countdown on a small transistor radio way past my bedtime. When older, it enabled me to smoke pot with the extractor fan on.

It was a really nice area to grow up in. If you've ever seen *Uncle Buck*, the first two *Home Alone* movies, *Planes, Trains and Automobiles* or *Ferris Bueller's Day Off* (five of my absolute favourite films), then you have an idea of the kind of street we lived on. *Ferris Bueller* gives you a good sense of how cool the city of Chicago is too, not just the suburbs (Ferris lived just near where I grew up), and as a bonus they also visit Wrigley Field, home of the Chicago Cubs.

Our house was always full of the sound of music, of talk about politics, movies, TV and the fate of the local Chicago Cubs baseball team, always perennial losers in those days (they went on to win the World Series in 2016). Long before my obsession with rock 'n' roll, I was fed a steady diet of Broadway musicals which dominated our family turntable. My parents would occasionally fly to New York City and leave me and my sister at home with a sitter. Consequently New York became this magical place where Broadway was king. They'd return with all these stories of the shows they'd seen bringing back the theatre programmes, those classic yellow and black *Playbill*s, for me to devour. I was captivated.

It all seemed so exciting and glamorous.

Eventually they took me and my sister to the Big Apple. I must have been about nine years old. We drove – it was about 800 miles – and broke up the journey by staying overnight in a Howard Johnson's motel in Ohio. I can still see the orange and turquoise logo. It was a thrill.

We were staying at my uncle's apartment in New York as he was away. He was an actor who had small bit parts in several TV sitcoms and also acted in regional theatre, while his wife Eileen was an opera singer. I found her showbiz manner totally engaging. To me, she was an incredibly exotic character, like no one I had met before.

I remember my parents telling us repeatedly to be careful in NYC, and no sooner had we gone out walking on our very first full day in the city than some shady character ripped the bottom part of my doll-shaped purse, so I was carrying around the head with no bottom and nothing in it without even knowing. We all thought it was hysterical. Happy days.

That's when I saw my first Broadway show, the classic *Gypsy*, starring one of America's greatest ever musical theatre stars, Ethel Merman. Looking back on it, the show is quite risqué for young kids, as the Gypsy in question is a stripper. But it really is quite an endearing love story with lyrics by the then relatively unknown Stephen Sondheim. Years later I would become a massive fan and eventually meet him over drinks in his New York City home with Rufus Wainwright. Seeing the show was just an incredible experience. However, the two main characters do not marry at the end and I left the theatre in tears.

New York played a massive role in our lives, as did the theatre. My mother was an actress in regional summer theatre when she met my dad and as we got older she started teaching drama to students. One of the musicals we loved was *The Pajama Game* – no wonder, as it's about unions and my dad was a union lawyer. One of the songs from the show was called 'Once-a-Year Day' and my parents decided to incorporate the concept into our lives. So once every year I could do whatever I wanted (within reason) with one parent while my sister did same with the other. The following year we'd alternate. Baseball games with Dad; the Art Institute with Mom. We really looked forward to these days almost as much as Thanksgiving and Christmas.

Around the age of sixteen my Once-a-Year Day became more adventurous as Mom and I went to New York City on our own. We walked so much we had to take our shoes off and saw as many Broadway shows as we could. It gave me a taste for big-city living which I have never outgrown. There's something so satisfying about having everything and anything in the arts, sports or restaurants within easy reach. I wouldn't want it any other way.

Even more memorable was a family trip to NYC a few years later after I graduated high school in 1970. No sooner had we arrived than I read in the *New York Times* that the Who were playing *Tommy* over the weekend at the Metropolitan Opera House. I was absolutely desperate to go but the shows were completely sold out. However, there was a Sunday matinee and my parents, after much heated discussion, finally relented and let me try my luck at getting a standby ticket. We were flying back to Chicago that night but off I went and stood in line, beyond excited at the prospect of getting in. As the clock crept closer to the 2.30 start time I was the second person in line when I heard the box office attendant tell the guy in front of me there was one ticket. Unbelievably he declined as he needed two and up I stepped, literally shaking, heart beating like crazy. All along I'd assumed if I was lucky enough to get a ticket it would be in the last row right up the top of the balcony, but I didn't care.

Even at that young age I was spoilt. I spent most of my money on concert tickets. Throughout junior high and high school, I had part-time jobs, and earning my own money gave me an early sense of independence. I spent lots of time and energy, when I should have been in class, booking tickets the minute they went on sale (there were no computers then) at the local record store or on the phone.

I eagerly paid for the ticket and in I went. I'd never been to the Met before – one of the most beautiful opera houses in the world. I had never seen the Who live either, so it was something of a massive double whammy. I'd only seen them in the film of Woodstock, which had taken place the summer before. I must have seen that film at least five times in various stages of pot-fuelled delight. If we had nothing to do on the weekend, my friends and I would go see *Woodstock*, sitting in the front row and pretending we were actually there.

You can only imagine my shock when the ticket ended up being in the twentieth row, centre, on the main floor. I didn't even have time to get used to my surroundings as no sooner had I taken my seat then the lights went down and the Who came on, playing *Tommy* from start to finish in all its glory, and then the set that was their incredible *Live at Leeds* album. I could barely catch my breath before I had to run back to the hotel to meet the family, full of adrenaline and unadulterated rock 'n' roll energy. I was high for days on the excitement of the show. It's all I talked about the whole flight back to Chicago. It remains one of the best shows I've ever seen. And I've seen a lot of great shows.

Long before my rock 'n' roll indoctrination, I was trans-fixed by musicals. It was a golden era: *West Side Story, My*

Fair Lady, *The Sound of Music*, *Oliver!* and countless others dominated the family turntable, along with a very worn copy of *The Andy Williams Christmas Album*. I loved Andy Williams and his weekly show was a family favourite too. We even liked the Osmond brothers. There was a fair amount of Ella Fitzgerald, Frank Sinatra, Barbra Streisand and just classic songs that we'd always sing around the house. Not that we were the von Trapps or anything, but we loved a good tune even though I personally couldn't carry one. Back then a lot of the big musicals became even bigger films a couple of years after opening on Broadway. The films of *West Side Story*, *The Sound of Music* and *Oliver!* were all classics that we enjoyed in the movies too.

My parents continued going to New York City throughout my adolescence and into adulthood, keeping me entertained with first-hand accounts of *Company*, *A Little Night Music* and *Sweeney Todd*. They also saw a lot of drama, especially by British playwright Harold Pinter, a rising Broadway star then. Pinter drove my parents crazy, and they would often argue about the true meaning of the play – for example, did the chair really represent a chair? Talk about theatre of the absurd.

My love of all things British manifested itself early on with a genuine fondness for Anthony Newley's musical *Stop the World – I Want to Get Off*, *Oliver!* and of course *Mary Poppins*, from which we knew every single song, having seen the film more than once and played the record till we wore it out.

There was also *Beyond the Fringe* – my parents had seen this acerbic British revue in New York with Peter Cook, Dudley Moore, Alan Bennett and Jonathan Miller and they'd bought the cast album. I couldn't have been older than ten but I loved the satirical British wit and played the album continuously. I also loved another satirical political revue popular at the time on TV: *That Was the Week That Was* with David Frost. Even at such a young age, I devoured all of that smart, spiky British humour. So by the time the Beatles arrived, I was more than ready.

I still vividly recall Antonioni's 1966 classic film *Blow Up* whose main character was a photographer played by David Hemmings. It was all about swinging London, though very dark, and provided another glimpse into a life that fascinated me.

Before the Beatles explosion, folk music was big and I was very keen on Peter, Paul and Mary (they turned the US on to Dylan), the New Christie Minstrels, the Kingston Trio and the Chad Mitchell Trio. Some of these artists were quite political, which meshed well with my growing interest in news and current affairs, something that was constantly reinforced during family dinner conversations.

The Beatles arrived in January 1964, and not a minute too soon as the country was still grieving from the assassination of President John F. Kennedy on 22 November 1963. I still remember that day as if it was yesterday. My teacher, Mrs Evans, had abruptly left the classroom only to return minutes later in floods of tears. She managed to regain enough composure to inform us that the president had been shot and killed. We were immediately sent home to our traumatised parents and there was no school for several days as the nation mourned. For us kids, it was the first time most of us had experienced any kind of tragedy. It was the first time we had seen our parents grief-stricken.

During Kennedy's time in office, the US almost went to war because of the Cuban Missile Crisis. And I remember my mother being so scared that she bought a new pair of shoes to ease the pain, something I would repeat later when

I was older. There's nothing like a bout of retail therapy to cheer you up.

A mood of real sadness pervaded the country for months during what was usually the happiest time of the year: Thanksgiving and Christmas. Then barely three months on from this seismic event, something incredibly joyous happened to American youth: the arrival of the Beatles. Their first album came out in January 1964, and soon after I brought it to school for our weekly 'show and tell'. No one had brought an album in before. It was the first album I had actually bought myself with the weekly pocket money my parents gave me. This was quickly followed by the Beatles' American television debut on *The Ed Sullivan Show*. Ed had a must-see Sunday night variety show which always featured a schizophrenic mix of magicians, ventriloquists, comics, clowns and musicians. Ed was astute when it came to music and gave lots of performers their first break, including the Beatles.

It felt like every household in the country sat glued to their small black-and-white TV when the Beatles were on. And subsequently Ed Sullivan had everyone on: the Stones, the Dave Clark Five, the Hollies, Herman's Hermits, the Animals – the whole of what came to be known as the British Invasion.

A year later the pop music show *Shindig* arrived, quickly followed by *Hullabaloo*. These were US versions of *Ready Steady Go!* and I'd rush home from school to watch, along with the more traditional Dick Clark's *American Bandstand*.

It wasn't just a golden era for music on TV, it was a golden age for American sitcoms. My favourite was *The Dick Van Dyke Show*, which ran from the autumn of 1961 for four glorious seasons. Written by Carl Reiner, the main characters were writers for a TV show and Dick was the head writer.

It was set in New York City and Dick's wife was played by Mary Tyler Moore. Each week they had to write the monologue for the show's star and were often stuck for ideas. It was so smart, clever and ahead of its time. More importantly, it made a huge impression on me, further cementing my growing desire to write for a living.

Although I can't sing a note, I wasn't a bad musician as a kid. I started playing clarinet when I was about eleven and took lessons in our wood-panelled family den every Saturday morning with a teacher called Ben Bailys, who also taught music at my school. He was one hep cat, as they might have said back then, and always wore a sharp suit. Like my opera-singing Aunt Eileen, he represented showbiz glamour to my adolescent eyes. No doubt he was the coolest person I had ever met. It was like he lived on another planet.

I was part of the school band for a good few years, the highlights of which were the annual concerts and the local parades on Memorial Day or the Fourth of July around our Norman Rockwell-esque village of Glencoe, with my parents proudly waving from the sidewalk.

At some point, encouraged by Ben Bailys, I took up the saxophone (obviously inspired by the Dave Clark Five), which led to me forming my first and only group, the Demi Semi Quavers, which is the musical term for thirty-second note. We wore granny dresses and granny glasses. It was 1966 and I was in eighth grade, my last year of what was called junior high. I had cards printed up that said: 'Hire us now, it'll be too late when we're famous'. Even then a showbiz career beckoned. A friend of my mom's worked at the *Chicago Tribune* and she commissioned an article about us, complete with a photo shoot. We hadn't even done a proper gig yet but we had a huge feature in the daily paper, planting the seeds of how PR works in my brain. After a couple of months' rehearsal and the occasional live show at a community centre, we broke up.

Despite the fact that I can't hold a tune, I could read music and took up acoustic guitar. You could find me nightly in my room, happily picking out show tunes and pop singles, excelling on the Animals' 'We Gotta Get Out of this Place'. Another favourite was 'Michelle' by the Beatles. I wore out that *Rubber Soul* songbook.

When I started high school at New Trier East, I assumed I would continue with my music education. But the first day I walked into class and saw the students, who in my opinion were not in any way, shape or form what I would call 'cool', I knew this wasn't for me so I called it a day and quit, happy to pursue a more exciting social life. To my teenage way of thinking, cool was the way to go.

Since junior high I'd always had a part-time job, first at the Glencoe library filing books, and then the best job ever, at Wally King's Record Shop every Saturday and more frequently in the summer. Being paid to suggest records people should buy and file new releases away was heavenly, and Mr and Mrs Wally King were sweethearts. Later, while at university, I had a summer job at a women's clothing store and worked at the wrap desk where I could listen to music all day long while wrapping presents or packages. It was the summer of 1972 and all I played was the Rolling Stones' *Exile on Main Street*, which to this day remains my favourite album, featuring my favourite ever single, 'Tumbling Dice'.

High school was everything I hoped it would be. It was an exciting time to be growing up in the world. Luckily for me, I was the only one among my friends who could roll joints, so they would give me their small bag of pot and ask me to roll the joints for them and of course I would keep some for myself. Very enterprising, even then. Record sleeves were good for many things, and providing a surface to roll joints on was one of them.

Getting my driving licence at sixteen opened up a whole new range of possibilities to see live music. Prior to that I had to depend on my parents to drive me to see a concert. One Christmas I bought my sister tickets to see Herman's Hermits, even though she didn't even like them, just so I could see the support act, the Hollies.

In the summer the Chicago Symphony frequently played at Ravinia, a beautiful sprawling arts complex with an outdoor theatre and seats on the lawn where thousands of people would picnic. They had many popular concerts as well as the symphony and I spent much of my high school and college summers going to Ravinia with friends and family. It was such a special place and so close to our home.

An entire lifestyle began to form around the culture of pop music and I was totally smitten. Late in 1967 *Rolling Stone* was founded and I think I pretty much bought it from the start. It's hard to explain now to those who have grown up with the internet and everything online but in those days newspapers and magazines were the only places you could read about music. You had to go to a record store to buy records, or vinyl as it is now called. And you could listen to them in-store. There were record stores everywhere, and inside these magical places it felt like a members' club, with everyone, even the staff, enamoured with music. If you've ever seen Jack Black playing the obsessive record-store employee in the film version of Nick Hornby's *High Fidelity*, you know what I'm talking about. You could kill hours just flipping through all the new releases, studying the album cover artwork, listening to whatever one was playing over the speaker system, requesting another, ordering albums they didn't have or even asking advice. Quite a few of the bigger stores even sold concert tickets and music magazines. The top 20 singles were even sold in grocery stores. Music was everywhere.

It was a burgeoning culture that kept expanding at a rapid pace. This was an extremely joyous time to discover new music, and the music just kept on coming. It wasn't just the actual music, the lyrics played their part too and many of these artists, especially singer-songwriters, helped us cope with all the problems associated with transitioning from adolescence to adulthood.

Much of my fascination with the UK came from all the amazing talent the country kept producing. England had it all, while the US seemed to trail far behind. England had the Beatles and the Stones, the Who and the Kinks. We had Jay and the Americans, Paul Revere & the Raiders, the Association (two great singles: 'Along Comes Mary' and 'Windy'), and the wonderful Mamas and Papas. The Beach Boys were probably the first American group to try to rival some of Britain's finest.

These groups were on a creative jag like nothing before or since. It's why these albums are timeless and sound as good today, if not better, than they did when they first came out. It's why they keep selling to one generation after another. The Beatles had a run of albums that is simply staggering: *Revolver* (1966), *Sgt. Pepper's Lonely Hearts Club Band* ('67), the White Album ('68) and *Abbey Road* ('69).

And they weren't the only ones. How's this for a four-album sequence from the Rolling Stones: *Beggars Banquet* ('68), *Let It Bleed* ('69), *Sticky Fingers* ('71) and *Exile on Main Street* ('72). Its mind-boggling.

The Kinks, a band who just don't get enough credit, fronted by Ray Davies, a pure genius, a songwriter whose depiction of everyday English life has no equal, gave the world this five-album cycle: *Face to Face* ('66), *Something*

Else ('67), *The Kinks Are the Village Green Preservation Society* ('68), *Arthur (Or the Decline and Fall of the British Empire)* ('69) and *Lola Versus Powerman and the Moneygoround* ('70).

And don't even get me started on double-sided singles, where the Beatles reigned supreme. For something like a dollar you could get: 'We Can Work It Out' / 'Day Tripper' (probably the greatest double A-sided single *ever*), 'Penny Lane' / 'Strawberry Fields Forever' and 'Hey Jude' / 'Revolution'.

It was all very accessible and easy. You'd read about new bands and artists in *Rolling Stone, Creem, Crawdaddy* and *Hit Parade*, then go out and buy the music – from San Francisco bands (Jefferson Airplane, Grateful Dead) to LA's Laurel Canyon singer-songwriters (Jackson Browne, Joni Mitchell, Byrds) and of course Dylan. My party piece when I'd had a few too many was, for some reason, to sing all the verses (and it's a *long* song) of Dylan's 'It's Alright, Ma (I'm Only Bleeding)'. It's incredible now to think that the album it was on, *Bringing It All Back Home*, came out in 1965 and sounds as good today as it did then.

Bob Dylan had an incredible string of classic albums too. *Bringing It All Back Home* was followed the same year (!) by *Highway 61 Revisited*, the following year by the double album masterpiece *Blonde on Blonde*, followed in '67 with a complete change of direction with the the country-tinged *John Wesley Harding*.

In those days, creativity literally knew no bounds.

Much of this music was also deeply political, and by 1968 when I turned sixteen, a lot of our initial optimism had disappeared, as world events darkened our rather idyllic outlook. In April of that year the great civil rights leader Martin Luther King was assassinated, an event that caused an incredible amount of unrest around the country. It culminated that summer in Chicago with the Democratic Convention when the streets were taken over by anti-Vietnam War protesters, some of whom became notorious as the Chicago Seven. I'd only just got my driving licence that year and when the trouble erupted my parents wouldn't let us anywhere near the city. A sense of reality suddenly interurpupted our day-to-day lives. Those were dark times, and when Nixon was elected that November, the mood turned sombre.

As much as I loved New York, Chicago was home and it remains one of America's great cities. It has none of the snobbery of New York or LA, and the people are far friendlier. It's a great sports and music town too, with baseball, hockey and NFL football all represented, and any band who toured the States always played Chicago no matter how small the tour. It remains famous for the best hot dogs (mustard essential) in the US, and invented deep-dish pizza. And it lay, in all its glory, beside that beautiful, expansive Lake Michigan. In almost every way, it was my kind of town.

It's no surprise that I was good at writing and debating. I briefly joined the debating club but it was too demanding a schedule, conflicting with time I could have spent listening to music and smoking pot. And just like music class, I didn't feel the other students were my kind of people. I liked to think of myself as cool, which was not a word that could describe anyone in the debating club. My father regularly wrote briefs for his court cases and would read them to us. He was a trial lawyer and a damn good one, and I no doubt learnt from him how to defend myself, articulate my thoughts and just argue, as many a nightly dinner table conversation turned into a me vs. him thing – mostly in the nicest possible way though occasionally it got heated. We both wanted to win.

I eventually started writing for my high school newspaper – the *New Trier News* – and had my own column during my senior year. When we returned to school after our summer break in September 1969, there was one kid who had been to Woodstock and we all looked at him with admiration and wonder, as if he'd been to the moon.

I must have always been attracted to writing as one of my earliest childhood memories was of a little printing press I was given as a birthday or Christmas present. My first crush was a doe-eyed boy called Stuart Shamen (what a rock-star name) who lived down the street. We used to make little newspapers up on this tiny ink printing press.

My columns were split evenly between reviews of live shows, albums or events (featuring Woodstock, the Band, Joe Cocker, Dylan, CSN&Y) and humorous takes on daily life at high school, the funniest of which was titled 'Exposition Is a New Found Art Form' written after seeing a man expose himself while on the way home from school, calling the police on arriving home (mobile phones did not exist) and eventually having to go to the station to identify a suspect. It was like being in a movie or a TV show. Or the column about the rising number of female washrooms in school being shut with the headline: 'Locked Washroom Problem: Where Do We Go Now?'

I graduated high school in June 1970 and decided to attend the University of Missouri because of their excellent school of journalism. And because I wanted an adventure somewhere different from where I'd grown up. My father drove me and all my worldly possessions to Columbia, Missouri and I remember making him listen to the Who's *Tommy* pretty much the whole way there, me singing all the words.

It was bittersweet when he drove off, and a little bit scary, leaving me standing outside my dormitory. But it was also exciting. A new chapter was about to begin.

Family dinner in Chicago, late 1960s
Left to right: Jan (sister), Shel Charone (Dad), BC,
Rose Charone (Mum)

Chapter 2
I'm On the Guest List!

Soon after I arrived at the University of Missouri, Jimi Hendrix died and a month later Janis Joplin. A growing sense of reality had suddenly reared its ugly head. The political landscape matched the sombre mood too. A dark cloud called Vietnam hovered over America while Nixon resided in the White House. The deaths of Hendrix and Joplin, soon followed by that of Jim Morrison (lead singer of the Doors), added to the general feelings of discontent that coloured our move into adulthood. We took it personally.

These were turbulent times politically, and university was a great place to be witnessing them. Discussions were always free flowing and challenging. Luckily the exuberance of youth kept me positive and enthusiastic about what lay ahead. I refused to get weighed down by the prevailing negativity.

Columbia, Missouri was a typical American college town dominated by the mostly student population. The town's main record store was the centre of my universe and it's where I spent any spare cash I had on my constantly expanding record collection. Reading about music and buying music occupied most of my free time. It was a provincial, Middle American, small-town existence which made me appreciate Chicago even more. I quickly realised I was built for the big city and wanted everything on my doorstep.

Not that I was homesick, far from it; I was city sick, missing going to all those shows in Chicago. The friends in my dorm were nice enough but I didn't make any lasting friendships and it soon became apparent that I would not do more than my freshman year there.

It didn't help that my initial overtures to work on the school paper were instantly rebuffed. I wasn't really pursuing my journalistic dreams and so I applied for sophomore year at Northwestern University, attractively situated between my parents' house and the city. I had good grades at Missouri – because I could write I always tested well, finishing exams when others were still struggling with an outline – and was accepted as an English major. To major in journalism would have meant starting over again and losing first-year credits, and I was in way too much of a hurry to finish up and start life to do that.

After freshman year ended, my parents took the family to Europe. It was summer 1971, and this trip of a lifetime cemented everything I had hoped and dreamt England would be. Our itinerary kicked off in London, then took in Liverpool and Dublin and finished off in Paris. My dad often spoke at American Bar Association Conventions – nothing to do with alcohol but a prestigious American organisation of lawyers. They were having their annual convention in London so my parents generously thought it would be a wonderful opportunity for us all to experience Europe for the first time together.

We stayed at the Grosvenor House on Park Lane as that's where the convention was based, a lovely five-star hotel across from Hyde Park. One night I wandered off, no doubt to go see some music, while my sister took a cab back to the wrong Grosvenor House Hotel, in Victoria, and I got into big trouble with my parents for that particular escapade.

Truth be told, I was too old to go on holiday with my parents any more, now a soon-to-be college sophomore at the no longer adolescent age of nineteen. There was many a painful moment when Dad had us posing for family photos outside Buckingham Palace or the Louvre, me dying of embarrassment. There was no doubting, however, that I was one lucky lady to get to experience Europe in all its splendour and I eagerly drank it all in.

I practically cried when walking over Waterloo Bridge, having devoured all the classic Kinks songs, especially 'Waterloo Sunset'. Once I moved to the UK, I actually visited Muswell Hill where the Kinks were born, tracking down the pub on the sleeve of their classic *Muswell Hillbillies* album. Once, giddy with excitement, I'd even spotted Ray Davies in the foyer of the west end theatre where the musical *Applause* was playing.

Suddenly all the places I'd seen on TV and in the movies and heard about on record were there in the flesh. Those inimitable red double-decker buses really did exist, as did the iconic red post boxes. America is such a new country compared to the UK and I was fascinated by its history and tradition.

I had a tendency to be a bit gullible, and my family often took full advantage of this. When we drove into Liverpool, I was beside myself with excitement. And as we approached the city, someone shouted: 'Look, there's a sign that says home of the Beatles.' But of course no such sign existed though no doubt it does now. It was the romantic in me, always wanting to believe. Never lose that child in you.

After returning home, the rest of summer sped by and soon I was ensconced in my new digs, a really nice dormitory with no roommate right in the centre of the beautiful

Northwestern campus. Classes were good, though I could not get the hang of astronomy – you had to take a science to get your degree – and smoking a joint before class certainly didn't help though the stars sure looked pretty. It was a miracle I passed.

Motivated by our European adventures, I decided I wanted to go to London to do what was commonly known then as junior year abroad and became obsessed with the idea. Sadly, Northwestern had no such programme in London but a very good east coast university, Tufts, had one for English and drama majors. Even better, Northwestern accepted the junior-year credit without having to take any kind of test on returning. Competition for places was fierce and I was on complete tenterhooks till that acceptance letter came through the post.

Northwestern is in Evanston, which is a proper city, not like the suburbs that decorated what was called the North Shore where my parents lived and where I went to high school. The city centre boasted a really great record store called Laurie's which became my second home. It was a microcosm of life back then; the atmosphere was contagious. You were spending time with like-minded strangers and it felt great. That same feeling carried on to live concerts – you felt like you were with family, all enjoying a journey of discovery with each and every new artist you saw in concert. The excitement in the hall was palpable.

When our family visited New York City, I couldn't wait to visit the Sam Goody record store. I'd grown up seeing their page ads for new albums in the Sunday *New York Times* and it didn't disappoint. Record stores were getting bigger and better as the industry grew, and the biggest of them all was undoubtedly Tower Records in LA. I'd seen photos of the store on Sunset with its giant album covers in the windows and its infamous red and yellow signage and couldn't wait to visit on the west coast. Years later I would spend hours in the shop and it wasn't unusual to see musicians browsing there. Sadly all that is history now, and all that remains is the red and yellow signage, the store all but a memory.

Every Thanksgiving the band Chicago – originally known as CTA in honour of the Chicago transport system – played a special show at the Auditorium Theatre and, as good as my mom's turkey dinner was, I couldn't wait to jump in the Mini Metro, light up a nice little joint, pick up a couple of friends and drive into the city for the show. They were similar to Blood, Sweat & Tears in that they both had a big horn section and meshed that sound with guitars. It was a heady mix.

I saw so many amazing concerts at the Auditorium Theatre, including the Doors (with the Staple Singers as support!), Joe Cocker, Derek and the Dominos (with Eric Clapton), Joni Mitchell, Traffic, and Crosby, Stills Nash & Young.

The group that really impressed me the most was the Band, a mostly Canadian outfit who rose to prominence backing Bob Dylan, most famously when he went electric. They were the first band I ever saw who refused to do any obligatory audience chat and never once bellowed 'HELLO, CHICAGO'. They didn't even speak, but boy could they play, swapping instruments with ease. It was a remarkable show in which they played their classic second album in its entirety. Impressive.

The capacity of the Auditorium was just under 4,000 and it was famous for its incredible acoustics. A national historical landmark, it reopened in 1967 just in time for me to get one hell of a musical education within its pristine walls. It was just off Michigan Avenue, not far from Orchestra Hall where the Chicago Symphony played, and close to the famous

Chicago Art Institute where we always went on school trips when I was younger. I can still remember the whole class standing in front of one of the most famous paintings in their collection, *A Sunday Afternoon on the Island of La Grande Jatte* by George Seurat. The entire painting is made up of what we kids would call dots but was referred to as the pointillist technique. Years later Stephen Sondheim would use that painting as the basis of his ground-breaking musical *Sunday in the Park with George*. Small world.

I spent a lot of time, energy and money making sure I had tickets the day they went on sale for all the good concerts. It was so much easier back then. No huge record company holds. Just first come, first served.

The Quiet Knight was a much smaller venue – a club, with tables and a bar. It was where I saw artists who were mostly just beginning their careers, some even before their debut albums came out. Here I was lucky enough to see Linda Ronstadt with what would become the Eagles as her backing band, Jackson Browne, John Prine (a Chicago native), and countless others, most of whom never made it big for that long. It was just as magical as the Auditorium Theatre and contributed hugely to my live-music education throughout my college years.

It was at one of the Auditorium Theatre concerts that I accosted Al Rudis, the music critic for the *Chicago Sun Times*. Meeting him no doubt changed my life as he politely listened to me babble on about wanting to be a rock critic and offered to consider any good ideas I had for a feature. The first piece I wrote was published and then a few more so it was no surprise that he offered to take anything good I could get while living in London.

I left for London early in September 1972. There were about forty students on the Tufts University programme and we all lived in a bed and breakfast off Gloucester Road. It was beyond the most exciting thing that had happened to me thus far. I met lots of interesting people and the classes were quite innovative. We had one at the Victoria and Albert Museum. It was a great area to live in and the best part of all, of course, was that I was actually living in London.

I set about taking in as much music as I could and through sheer tenacity somehow ended up at a press reception for Ravi Shankar at an Indian restaurant on Curzon Street in Mayfair. I'd been invited by his UK press officer, Moira Bellas, who worked at Kinney Records which owned Warner Brothers and Atlantic Records in Europe. I happened to mention that I was keen on seeing America – a CSN&Y-style band who were massive at the time having had a huge hit with the Neil Young-inspired song 'Horse With No Name'. They weren't doing any concerts but were soon to perform on *The Old Grey Whistle Test* and I was desperate to go.

Amazingly, Moira invited me to the taping of the show. I'd never been in a TV studio before so it was all very exciting. Even better, for some even more inexplicable reason, I was invited to join the band and the people who worked at the record label for what they called 'post-show food and drinks' at a Lower Sloane Street institution called the Mexicana. This was where record companies often took visiting American artists. At the time Mexican food was a rarity in London (to be honest, food in London back then left a lot to be desired) but the atmosphere was lovely, no doubt aided by the very strong tequila, also something of a novelty back then.

Many margaritas later Moira and I were best friends – and remain so today. I was subsequently invited to many of their shows and press receptions. The novelty soon wore off and this became a way of life which I embraced 100 per cent. A huge door opened and I was only too happy to walk through.

One contact leads to another and soon I was friendly with many other music PRs who were eager to get their acts in the *Chicago Sun Times*. I was interviewing many bands and had more than a few features printed in the paper, which was one way my parents could keep up with my exploits. My network of friends and contacts grew far beyond the kids back at the bed and breakfast. I began to meet many music paper writers who soon came to define the golden days of music journalism. I finally convinced *NME* to let me write for them. I probably just wore them down. It was easier to say yes and give me a chance than keep taking my endless calls! *NME was* the best of the bunch. I was making some money freelancing but my parents were very generous which enabled me to live in London when classes finished.

My Tufts programme ended in June so I moved into a flat and set about going to even more shows and receptions and just enjoying everything London had to offer. My fondest memories were of nights spent at the infamous Speakeasy Club on Margaret Street, eating the most delicious steak with mushroom sauce and peas while watching Keith Moon (the infamous original Who drummer) and other famous musicians let their hair down. It was a magical mystery tour come to life. Often up-and-coming bands would play and some of the famous musicians enjoying a night off would get up onstage and jam.

I flew home the day before my senior year was due to begin with a freelance job writing for *NME* as a US correspondent. I lived at home with my parents for my senior year as I had no desire to go back to a dorm and was spending a lot of time when not in class in the city. I've always had a great relationship with my parents and even called them regularly when I was in London. My sister had just started her freshman year at the University of Michigan so my parents were glad of the company. At least that's what they said. No doubt there was many a night where I'd stumble in just like Jennifer Saunders' character in *Absolutely Fabulous*, barely able to speak but happy as hell.

At some point during my senior year I'd seen that Bob Dylan was playing at my sister's school, the University of Michigan, so persuaded my parents that would be a great weekend to visit. There weren't too many nice hotels in Ann Arbor back then so it came as no surprise that Dylan was actually staying at the same hotel as we were. I was a massive Dylan fan. At one point I had a Dylan collage on my bedroom wall and I think I knew most of the lines in the classic D.A. Pennebaker film of his infamous 1966 UK tour, *Don't Look Back*, by heart. One afternoon during the visit I got in the elevator and, much to my complete and utter surprise, Bob Dylan was in the small lift. Heart pounding like mad, I rode all the way up to the top floor where he got out. It was unreal. I was giddy for days.

I met Dylan two other times, if you could call our first encounter a meeting. A couple of years later I was in New York City writing a *Crawdaddy* cover story on Eric Clapton, who was recording a track for what would be the Dylan album *Desire*. Just being in the studio with both those men was definitely a bucket-list experience at the time. It was surreal watching Clapton put his particular electric spin on Dylan's songs. Watching them interact was an education in itself and being in a recording studio with A-list musicians intoxicating.

The third meeting was the best. It was at the Savoy Hotel in London, visiting Keith Richards. Keith was in another room of the suite with his wife Patti and told me if there was a knock on the door to get it. Not long after, I opened the door and there, standing in the hall, was Bob Dylan and a woman wearing a leopard-skin pillbox hat. One of Dylan's most famous songs from the classic *Blonde on Blonde* album is called 'Leopard-Skin Pill-Box Hat' and I was practically speechless. The song just kept going through my head on speed dial. I barely managed to let them in, could hardly speak and miraculously got the words out: Keith won't be long.

Dylan was in London recording with Dave Stewart (of the Eurythmics) and when Keith did return he played us (well, I was in the room) a cassette with some new music. Keith often stayed at the Savoy and there were many nights over the years where I left the hotel in something of a fuzzy state of mind but nothing surpassed the insanely surreal excitement of that particular evening. The corridors all look the same and sometimes it was hard to find the elevator. And it's not just down to the drugs or the drink, it's the layout of the hotel. (Just last year I was there with Dave Grohl, who was promoting his *Storyteller* book. It took me ages to find the lift, let alone the suite. And I was completely sober!)

Senior year was quite liberating. I was lucky enough to have an incredible professor who would meet me for a beer once a week to talk about the books I was reading and discuss Raymond Chandler. By now my writing career was really exploding. I was a regular contributor to the excellent weekly *Chicago Reader*, reviewing concerts and doing interviews.

Life was very exciting but I was missing London so much that I went to visit Moira for my Christmas break that year. I even went to New York City to meet her when she was in town with some UK writers she had taken there to see the Doobie Brothers. We all went to Max's Kansas City one night, full of tequila sunrises, to see disco diva Sylvester. Those were the days.

By the time I graduated in June 1974, I was writing for the *NME*, the *Chicago Sun Times*, the *Chicago Reader* and had just started with *Rolling Stone*. I was a writer, a music critic, a journalist, chasing a dream that was fast becoming a reality. Summer sped by. My work permit from *Sounds* was sorted. Nixon resigned in early August after months and months of Watergate trials and tribulations, and shortly after I was off too. I was moving to London. And I couldn't wait.

Press reception at the Mexicana, Lower Sloane Street,
mid 1970s

Chapter 3
It's Only Rock 'n' Roll

The last piece I wrote for *NME* was a live review of Crosby, Stills, Nash & Young from Milwaukee, Wisconsin that ran in early August. The first piece I wrote for *Sounds*, in my new full-time position as staff writer, was a live review of CSN&Y from Wembley Stadium, London published a month later in September 1974 with the headline: 'By the Time We Got to Neasden', a parody on their famous hit 'Woodstock'. I always liked a bit of a joke.

They were completely different reviews from two totally different shows but the symmetry was neat. During my freshman year in Missouri I wrote a big paper on the social significance of the Who's *Tommy* and was very happy to reuse the same paper the following year at Northwestern. It seemed such a shame to let it go to waste.

I absolutely loved CSN&Y in any way, shape or form. They were really the first American supergroup who splintered early but were a fascinating case study in egos and success. Stephen Stills was the first artist I ever interviewed who I wished I hadn't, who fell so hard from the pedestal I had placed him on that I couldn't listen to his music for years. He was just plain nasty and seemed to me to have a chip on his shoulder so big it was a surprise he could get in the room. He was a genius though, and without him there would never have been that amazing CS&N debut album.

It was a great lesson for me to learn early, that just because someone was a famous musician, it did not necessarily mean they were a nice or good person. I also learnt early that, as the Lester Bangs character played by Philip Seymour Hoffman in the totally brilliant film *Almost Famous* says to the Cameron Crowe-inspired journalist: just remember, 'they are not your friends'.

I met Cameron Crowe more than a few times before and during my years at *Sounds*, most memorably when the Who played Madison Square Garden. He was really just starting out then but there was always something about him. He absolutely loved music in the same way I did and you could feel that in his writing. He went on to enjoy amazing success as the star writer for *Rolling Stone* and then of course in film as a director and screenwriter. Our paths crossed decades later at the Toronto Film Festival when we were both there with Pearl Jam, him for his work on the *PJ20* film and me as their UK PR with a bunch of writers in tow.

You'd be surprised how many people who work in the music business make the mistake of believing the artist is your friend. That's really where the trouble starts, and often ends in extreme sadness. I saw so many people try to copy the Stones' extracurricular habits and fall by the wayside, but more of that later. As an artist onstage and record, especially in the early days, Stephen Stills was magical. His first solo album was stellar, and his country-flavoured band Manassas had some depth and were terrific live. But the more I interviewed him, the less I liked him, and by the time I interviewed him at some scuzzy Holiday Inn somewhere nondescript in America's Midwest, I saw a harsh side to him and the self-hatred. Enough was enough.

Sounds was the first full-time office job I had, fresh out of university. The boys in the office could not have been nicer or more welcoming. It was a totally liberating experience. We were encouraged to write about the music we liked, though we were equally free to be as snide and cynical as we wanted about music we did not like. I must confess, though, to feeling a little guilty about an unnecessarily cruel review of the double album *Tales from Topographic Oceans* and quite possibly a couple of equally mean Rick Wakeman (Yes keyboard player) solo-album reviews. I also could not grasp the point of Pink Floyd's *The Wall* and had to gather all my inner strength just to last the course of the live show at Earl's Court. The music and presentation of the show was just anathema to everything I loved about rock 'n' roll.

Another smaller music paper, *Record Mirror*, shared our big office off the Holloway Road in Islington. We were literally around the corner from the Rainbow, an illustrious London venue in Finsbury Park that thrived from the mid-seventies till it closed in 1982. I saw quite a few memorable shows there, including Dr. John with Allen Toussaint and the Meters, Van Morrison, Little Feat, and Bob Marley and the Wailers.

Record Mirror was a precursor to *Smash Hits* – a wonderful pop bible that was massive throughout most of the eighties. *Sounds* was all about rock in every shape and form, plus folk, American singer-songwriters, pretty much any genre. I was working and socialising with like-minded people and being paid for it. It was in every way a dream job.

All my romantic notions of newspapers, deadlines and journalism came alive during those first heady days at *Sounds*. We had music on in the office all day long and travelled round Europe and the US on assignment often. When in the UK we lived it large at press receptions with full bars even at lunchtime – no such thing as just wine and beer back then. The concert halls and clubs were great. After all, we were on the guest list!

I was the only woman on the staff and something of a novelty in also being American. When I was in college, the only female writers I read in the music magazines at the time were Ellen Sander and Lisa Robinson. They were pretty much the only two women rock critics I knew of. Too often we were dismissed as groupies. Ellen's excellent collection *Trips* has been reprinted and is worth a read as it captures the heady days of that pre- and post-Woodstock US era really well.

Being an American in London was a big advantage and I suppose my bulldog personality helped me enjoy a successful career. The inbuilt confidence that Americans have stood out among the less outgoing Brits. This was particularly useful when interviewing apathetic pop stars. I think my true strength was the fact that I loved music and was extremely knowledgeable. And I really believe that the musicians appreciated this. I have always been and always will be incredibly enthusiastic. I imagine when you're stuck in a hotel room doing interviews all day, it's a welcome relief to speak to someone who actually likes the music. Years later when I became a PR, I applied the same attitude, to dizzying effect.

Access to artists back then was nowhere near what it isn't now. These days it's a straight forty-five minutes – if you're lucky – in a hotel room or record-company office. Or, worst case scenario, a phoner or email or a post-pandemic zoom. Back then you went to Eric Clapton's house and watched him drink Carlsberg Special Brew at 10 a.m. But you didn't write about it. There was a circle of trust that led to access.

Not that we didn't write the truth; we just didn't take advantage of artists personal traumas including drug or alcohol abuse.

One of the things I loved most about London, England and the whole of Europe was the history and the heritage. America was an incredibly young country and had nothing comparable to the architecture that London had. To this day, when I walk or drive over Waterloo Bridge I am awestruck at the beauty of it, the way St Paul's glistens at night. One of the great things about the suites Keith Richards used to have at the Savoy was that view of the river and the whole South Bank.

I lived in a basement flat on Sloane Street, towards the Sloane Square end, and just opposite Cadogan Gardens. It was an amazing location and a nice flat within walking distance of King's Road near, the legendary Chelsea Potter pub which the Stones used to frequent, not far from their original Edith Grove flat. I've always been lucky, and having this flat at the start to my new life could not have been better. I even had access to the private Cadogan Gardens.

At some point, probably eighteen months in, my friend got a girlfriend, and understandably it was time for me to move out. As luck would have it, I found a huge studio flat on the first floor of a building four doors down, with a very small outside space (you couldn't call it a balcony) overlooking Sloane Street. I didn't even need a moving van as we carried everything over. If walls could talk, the flat would have an awful lot of stories.

From London I was still writing a lot for *Rolling Stone*, which was the biggest music magazine in the world at the time. In addition to writing 3,000-word features for *Sounds*, reviewing at least two or three albums a week and a couple of live shows, my freelance career was soaring. Throughout my first eight months at *Sounds* I wrote features for *Rolling Stone* on a wide variety of artists from London: Kiki Dee (famous for a duet with Elton John); Genesis (I was a huge Peter Gabriel fan); Alvin Lee (former Ten Years After front-man, featured in Woodstock); the Faces (Rod Stewart was the lead singer, more to come on him soon); Ian Hunter (the fab Mott the Hoople frontman); and a mad group Jack Bruce (ex-Cream) had formed with former Rolling Stone guitarist Mick Taylor and jazz mistress Carla Bley. You can see by the sheer width and breath of the type of artists I was writing about that I was something of an enterprising all-rounder.

As if this wasn't enough, I started working for the excel-lent and well respected American monthly music magazine *Crawdaddy* (*Rolling Stone* was biweekly). My first feature was a Jack Bruce interview that ran in March 1975, followed in quick succession by features on Roger Daltrey, Leo Sayer and Eric Clapton. Obviously I had a good thing going with *Sounds* and would recycle some of the features for US publications. No harm in that. Music journalism was in its infancy then. These days that would never be allowed.

In the spring of 1975 I went to Munich, where the Rolling Stones were recording, to write a cover story for *Crawdaddy* which would precede the band's American tour. They were working at Musicland Studios on what would become the *Black and Blue* album and were also auditioning guitarists to replace Mick Taylor. Ron Wood, who I knew well from the Faces, would eventually get the job.

I had been promised an interview with Keith Richards and was really nervous about whether it would happen, as so much was riding on it, a cover story assignment being quite a big deal. I flew alone to Munich; no label person or

PR came with me. These days that would never happen. My contact was Ian Stewart, the legendary Stones piano player, roadie and everything in between. He was the most down-to-earth, shoot-from-the-hip man you could ever meet and the last person you would pick out of a line-up as someone who worked for the Stones. Affectionately known as Stu, he was really the glue that for a long time kept the band together. When he died in 1985, the band threw a raucous, joyous wake for him at London's 100 Club on Oxford Street where they played a incredible set and celebrated his life. It was a privilege to be there.

I had no reason to worry, as not only did Keith do the interview, but much to my delight, I met him at the studio and got to see the band record, which was probably the highlight of my life at that point. As ever he was an incredible interview – smart, funny, honest and charismatic.

A couple of months later I was in NYC to see the band's show at Madison Square Garden, which I was reviewing for *Sounds*. I asked the manager if I could say hi to Keith after the show and was told to go to the Essex House on Central Park South where the band were staying. There were barricades on either side of the entrance for the fans gathered outside but in I went, all of this a first-time experience for me, and was ushered up to Keith's suite. The *Crawdaddy* cover story was out and, having agreed to see me, I assumed Keith liked it. The first thing he said to me was: where do you get off writing we're gonna break up? Who gave you that idea? Who? He said this in a tone that while not threatening, was equally none too friendly. He was mad.

I had ended what was an otherwise excellent piece by writing: 'Time, however, waits for no one – not even the Rolling Stones. "This could be the last time / Maybe the last time / I don't know".' and ended the feature by saying every time they step onstage they are without doubt the best band in the world. But I had to put my hand up and apologise to the rather irate man sitting next to me. I had to admit that no one gave me that idea, I had just tried to be clever.

It was a tremendous lesson learnt the hard way and one that made me respect and appreciate Keith even more. The fact that this incredible musician and songwriter in the world's best and biggest band, who had only recently come offstage from a triumphant sold-out show at Madison Square Garden, was calling me out on some bogus end to an interview with him was mind-blowing. The fact that he actually read it and cared speaks volumes about the kind of person he is.

I'd been working for *Sounds* for less than a year, and already I was travelling the globe interviewing heroes and idols, and living it large. You really can't imagine what this was like. Most Americans back then didn't even have a passport and few left the state they grew up in. It had only been a year since I'd graduated from university and already my new life seemed comfortable, normal and exciting. I was obviously making friends in London but with all the travel started making lots of friends and contacts in New York City and LA: managers, record-company employees, other writers. One standout friend was Jane Rose who worked for the Stones manager Peter Rudge. It was exciting to share everything happening to me with all of them, and, of course, share the discovery of new music. And live shows, dinners, receptions, drink and recreational drugs.

In New York City lots of the music business people stayed at the old Gramercy Park hotel or the Mayfair on Columbus Circle, both great locations, though Gramercy Park was not the upmarket safe haven then that it is now. Whenever you went on a trip you always bumped into familiar faces in the bar at either of these hotels and of course most of the bands, except the really big ones who could afford to stay on Central Park South, stayed at these hotels too. The Kinks used to always stay at the Warwick Hotel on Sixth Avenue just down from Radio City and you would often find them in the cosy bar. LA was either the Sunset Marquis or the Continental Hyatt House, known affectionately as the Riot House due to an exceptional amount of rowdy, raucous rock-band behaviour, most successfully and notoriously exemplified by Led Zeppelin and Keith Moon.

The Sunset Marquis was on a leafy side street just off Sunset Boulevard. It was a bit shabby but had that Americana cool that anyone from anywhere other than LA was enamoured with. Bands and journalists would often stay together, hanging out by the pool or in the notorious Whiskey Bar till all hours. There was a genuine sense of camaraderie then between artists, managers, label people, writers, everyone involved in the process. It was like an exclusive fraternity. There was an innocence about it that was charming.

In London all upcoming bands stayed at the Columbia Hotel just off Bayswater Road. It was probably two-star and often entire bands would share one big room. It wasn't unusual to turn up for an interview and find half the lobby full of nodding-off budding rock stars.

It wasn't just the Stones I loved and regularly interviewed. I adored the Faces, Rod Stewart, the Kinks and especially the Who. My friend Moira Bellas had a great roster of lots of incredible American acts, including the Eagles, Linda Ronstadt, Jackson Browne, Little Feat, Dr. John and Emmylou Harris. I had interview access to them all when they came to London and often flew to the US to cover them for *Sounds*.

The Faces, with Rod Stewart as lead singer and Ron

Wood on lead guitar, were one of my favourites. They were much better live than on record and perhaps that's why their albums never really exploded. But onstage was another story and their Christmas concerts at London's Kilburn Gaumont State were the stuff of legend. Rod would make his entrance dressed extravagantly in leopard print or spandex or both, with a huge feather boa, parading down a staircase with all the rock 'n' roll swagger he could muster. And he could muster a lot.

Rod had also made a series of near-perfect solo albums that sat alongside his work with the Faces. I had my first and only *Rolling Stone* cover story on Rod Stewart (January 1977) when I covered his first solo European tour in Scandinavia. I remember writing, this time in *Sounds*: 'Sexuality has run amuck, men are called miss.' Rod had an incredibly outrageous, openly gay PR man called Tony Toon (real name), and to describe him as flamboyant would be a massive understatement. Like Rod himself, Tony Toon was tremendously entertaining and a real character. Going on tour with them was like nothing else. Rod and his entire entourage were very welcoming. As I'd written about him often, I was made to feel very welcome. More like a friend than a journalist. But back then that was nowhere near as unusual as it is now.

Rod always embraced the emerging camp persona that was becoming more and more prominent in late-seventies music and culture. He and Elton John pretended to feud, most often in the pages of *NME*, calling themselves Sharon and Phyllis.

Rod Stewart is one of the few stars who doesn't disappoint when you meet him even now, decades later. He's exactly how you imagine and hope he will be. He's practically the same offstage and onstage, the same in interview and in private. All the people around him in those early days of his career were characters, including his long-time tour manager Pete Buckland, who had T-shirts printed up with my sexuality quote that the road crew wore for the rest of the tour. They found it incredibly amusing.

The T-shirts were a way of flirting with the ongoing but not really spoken-about issues of sexuality. Back then, the word gay was used to describe someone who was a bit carefree. Rod always walked that engaging tightrope between straight and camp.

My first two years in the UK at *Sounds* were filled with one highlight after another. Paul McCartney and his wife Linda had their own band, Wings, and I was lucky enough to interview them at Abbey Road Studios when they were recording what would become the classic single 'Silly Love Songs' for their fifth Wings album. It ran as a *Crawdaddy* cover story in April 1976. Just walking across the infamous zebra crossing on Abbey Road as I made my way into the studio was unreal. It seems odd to look back on it now, as I live nearby and whenever I drive past, people are taking photos of themselves crossing that zebra crossing. Even odder, my company MBC now works with Apple, the Beatles' label, as their UK PR, and Abbey Road Studios is somewhere I have been on countless occasions. But back then, the twenty-four-year-old me had no idea what lay ahead.

A couple of years before, I'd been to see Wings in Oxford, on what was their first tour. When we arrived at the venue, we were told, much to my shock and total excitement, that Paul McCartney would speak to us scribes for a few minutes. For an American Beatles fan who never even saw the Beatles in concert (*A Hard Day's Night* and *Help!* were as far as I got), this was just too good to be true.

Not expecting any kind of interview, I had nothing to write or record on except a well-worn paperback copy of

Evelyn Waugh's classic *Scoop*, so I scribbled Paul's words of wisdom in the margins of the book. I wish I still had it now. Talk about life imitating art. *Scoop* is all about journalism. After the show there was a raucous after-party that came to a crashing end when guitarist Henry McCullough drunkenly smashed a massive winged ice sculpture in the entrance to the restaurant front. Not long after, he left the group.

One of the bands I wrote about a lot were the Who. Back then, solo albums from successful musicians who wanted to spread their wings outside of the band environment were in vogue, and the Who were no exception. I interviewed them – guitarist and songwriter Pete Townshend, singer Roger Daltrey and the late, great bassist John Entwistle, also affectionately known as the Ox – often. Due to the regularity of these chats you actually got to know the artists quite well. Sometimes, as in the case of John Entwistle, you would go to his house for the interview, or in the case of Roger Daltrey, to Shepperton Studios when he was filming (*Tommy, Lisztomania*). And they really seemed to appreciate the support we gave them in the paper for their solo projects.

The Who were one of the best live bands I have ever seen, and no doubt when drummer Keith Moon tragically died in September 1978, the band were never really the same force. Roger was an incredible frontman – who can forget his Woodstock, *Tommy*-era persona with his suede fringed jacket, throwing the microphone round and round like a man possessed. However, an extremely fragile bond existed between him and Pete Townshend, and we fans found this dichotomy (described best in the classic Who song 'Behind Blue Eyes') fascinating. I was quite friendly for a time with another Who obsessive, *Crawdaddy* assistant editor John Swenson, and many a night we would stay up late when I was in New York, poring over hidden meanings in Who songs. It was all part of the fun.

At this point I must confess that by now I had developed quite a fondness for cocaine. It was everywhere, the quality was great, it wasn't too pricey and it certainly aided communication between us scribes and rock stars. It helped break down invisible walls and if used sparingly could be enormous fun. They say everything in moderation is best but it was hard to not go that one step beyond. It was part of the furniture in those days and seemed to be everywhere. Looking back on it now, I am probably the last person who needed that confidence boost that cocaine gives you. I was not shy, was always eager to express my opinion and not at all inhibited. It was just part of the scenery and fuelled all sorts of mischief.

Roger Daltrey enjoyed a successful solo career; his first two solo albums did well and I had interviewed him often. Still I was unprepared when he burst into tears when discussing his struggles with Pete during one such chat and I loved him even more for it. It was this kind of personal relationship that really made this era of journalism unique, something never to be repeated. The intensity of the rivalry between band members (and the Who were hardly the exception) was extraordinary. A piece about this printed in *Creem* had the headline 'Daltrey Responds to Townshend Interview', as if it was breaking news.

All great bands seem to feature a tense dynamic between the two main creatives that teeters on the edge of destroying or making them. It's something we writers and fans found so fascinating. The Kinks had it with brothers Ray and Dave Davies and of course the Stones have it with Mick and Keith. They walk that line between exploding and imploding and when they get in right, and the two worlds create rather than collide, the results are staggering.

During the summer of '76 the Who played a series of stadium shows across the UK and so I found myself one steamy night in June at their Glasgow Parkhead show (home of Celtic football club). Up-and-coming LA band Little Feat were on the bill, and I'd interviewed them a couple of times. Lowell George, the creative mainstay of the group and author of many amazing songs, the best known of which is probably 'Willin'' due to the Linda Ronstadt cover, invited me to hang out in his room after the show, primarily to try to finish off a huge stash of cocaine he had with him before he and the band flew to Amsterdam the next day. Sometime around 5 a.m., brains totally fried from drugs, in one of those hazy, coke-fuelled cotton-mouth states of joyous confusion, the hotel fire alarm went off. We assumed it was let off by either Keith Moon or one of the road crew and were later proved right. Lowell and I looked at each other and laughed, and no doubt had another line. Those were crazy times.

Not everything had a happy ending and my relationship with the Eagles was a case in point. I was an avid Jackson Browne fan from the early days and loved the Eagles from the start – their first hit was the Jackson-penned 'Take It Easy'. I saw them live and interviewed them in 1974 around the time their third album, *On the Border*, came out. They were great live and lovely guys to interview, all football T-shirts and puppy-dog enthusiasm for music, loving the life of being a rock star and everything it entailed.

A couple of years later I was flown to LA where they were doing promo for their classic *Hotel California* album. I was to interview Glenn Frey and Don Henley, the creative linchpins of the group, at the very swanky Beverly Hills Hotel, immortalised forever on the album sleeve. The minute I entered their suite I was immediately struck by the sense of change in them – boyish enthusiasm replaced by jaded cynicism. They kept going to the bathroom, and left traces of coke on the back of the toilet cistern – none too clever. Someone from the record company also taped the interview, something of a first for me and yet another sign of a change in them. It was a new dawn and suddenly one where we were on different sides. An invisible line separated the space between them and us. In the old days, we probably would have shared the drugs. Now it was a badly kept secret.

I wrote a piece on the band for *Sounds* and months later a *Crawdaddy* cover story. I was appalled when I saw the issue, as the cover illustration pictured the band in a car that had crashed with the headline 'Life in the Fast Lane', a totally bad-taste play on their massive hit of the same name for a track that appeared on the *Hotel California* album. The cover art had nothing whatsoever to do with me and I didn't even know about it till I saw a finished issue. Not surprisingly their manager, Irving Azoff, was apoplectic, telling Moira Bellas that I was not to be allowed into the UK when the Eagles played there. However, even Irving couldn't prevent me from entering the country I called home. I'd also planned on seeing them in Greensboro, North Carolina with an American friend from the UK who'd moved back there but when I arrived I was notified that there was no way I would be allowed into the show and should leave the state immediately.

Reading the piece back now, it has its snide moments but it's basically a good, positive, serious feature about the band. It was the cover illustration that was the problem and I was blamed for it. I felt awful. Years later when I worked at Warner Brothers, the late Timothy White, then editor of *Billboard*, visited our offices. He'd previously been on staff at *Crawdaddy* before becoming a star writer at *Rolling Stone*.

He remembered the ill-fated Eagles *Crawdaddy* cover and I happened to mention that manager and band still felt wounded and blamed me. Timothy promised to write to Irving absolving me of all blame for the cover illustration and he was as good as his word.

The drama intensified when drummer Don Henley had a massive solo hit with 'Boys of Summer' and while visiting London for a promo trip, complained bitterly in interviews about me, which was ridiculous. Obviously he couldn't let it go. Years later I did the press for a Don Henley solo album and took some UK press to LA for a promo trip and met up with both Don and Irving. At last I was forgiven.

My biggest regret as a writer involves Bruce Springsteen. His first couple of albums had totally passed me by, but by summer '75 there was a lot of noise about him and I went to a showcase at the hip New York City venue the Bottom Line. Before the show I had a short interview with Bruce. I can remember him sitting on the stairwell backstage, going through the motions for a chat with a writer who clearly hadn't done their homework. That writer was me. Why I wasn't prepared, who knows – it was out of character and the irony is that a couple of years later, round the time that *Darkness on the Edge of Town* came out, I became a massive fan.

By the time Bruce released his career-defining double album *The River*, I was borderline obsessive. He and his incredible E Street Band played six shows at London's Wembley Arena, all of them over three hours long. And I went every night. I also went to Birmingham and Manchester. They were glorious shows, full-blown examples of music at its most joyous and uninhibited, and the feeling throughout the sold-out crowd was equally contagious. It was a celebration of music at his most potent.

At the same time, Prince had come to London, armed with his breakthrough *Controversy* album, and was playing two shows at the Lyceum. I made a massive mistake by not going to one of the Prince shows (they fell on the same nights Bruce was at Wembley), which I still regret, but you can't undo the past. At least I made up for it on subsequent tours.

By autumn of 1976 I had become restless with churning out so many articles for *Sounds* and US magazines and wanted to write a book, something more lasting and permanent. Punk was just round the corner, and it just wasn't for me. I was enamoured with more mainstream music and didn't really relate to this soon-to-be next big thing. I could feel the sea change fast approaching and began to feel it was time to move on from being a rock critic. It was sign that one part of my career was ending and another door opening.

My first choice of subject was the Who, and though Roger was all for it, in the end Pete was not, so I moved on to the Stones and Keith Richards. Earlier that year the Stones toured the UK and I flew to Glasgow to see them play a couple of nights at the Apollo, a small former cinema. It was an unbelievable experience to see them in front of such an intimate crowd who ecstatically sang all the lyrics back at the band. It was like being at a football match. After the show I went back to the swanky Turnberry Hotel, where the band were staying, for interviews with Mick and Keith. I remember coming out of one of the band suites long after the sun came up and walking along the Ayrshire coast behind the hotel in a daze.

The Stones also played a massive outdoor show that summer at Knebworth and I wrote more than a few *Sounds* covers on the band. By this point I had a good relationship with Keith Richards having interviewed him on numerous occasions. There were two other UK journalists close to Keith at that time, Nick Kent and Pete Erskine, both of whom wrote for the *NME* and both of whom took the lifestyle a bit too far. I eventually asked Keith if I could do a book on him, and much to my surprise and delight he said yes. Even in those drug-fuelled years, I'm sure he realised that there was a far greater chance of me actually writing the book and getting it published than the other two. Sadly, Pete died all too young but Nick Kent remains one of the great UK music journalists of that era.

It's hard to believe now but back in '76 the world looked at the Rolling Stones principally as a vehicle for Mick Jagger. Keith was very much seen as something of an afterthought. He'd had more than a few brushes with the law and was probably better known for his bad-boy behaviour than his incredible ability to write a classic tune, play an amazing solo or hold the band together onstage and in the studio.

Keith lived outside Chichester in a quite magical house called Redlands in West Wittering. The house had an actual moat around it ('my best friend he shoots water rats' from the classic 'Live With Me', is a quite accurate description of Keith). The main open living room is surrounded by an upstairs gallery, and the wooden beams give it a really comfy feel. I'd been down to the house a few times and on one of those visits Keith suggested that I come to Toronto early in 1977 for the Rolling Stones shows at the El Mocambo club. It was the only thing on the band's schedule that year so it made sense to start the book then. I flew to Toronto at the end of February, on the same BA flight as Charlie Watts, though not in the same section of the plane. I had taken all of *Sounds'* petty cash float with me, for expenses, not knowing that I would never return to the office. I was excited to see the show and start the book. Little did I know what lay ahead. But soon the whole world would know too.

Backstage with Keith Richards, late 1970s

Chapter 4
Sing Me Back Home

The Royal Canadian Mounted Police reached the thirty-second floor of Toronto's Harbour Castle Hotel before I did, arresting Keith for possession of heroin. Days earlier his partner Anita Pallenberg had been arrested at the airport for possession of hash and a mysterious blue pill when she and Keith landed with their seven-year-old son Marlon. She was later fined $400 and let off for the blue Tic Tac.

But Keith was in big trouble. Suddenly rehearsal time for the upcoming club shows was cut short by meetings with lawyers and court appearances. Keith was no stranger to the law but this was his most serious drug charge yet, with a prison sentence a very real possibility. Back in 1967 he was infamously arrested at Redlands along with Mick Jagger (remember Marianne Faithfull and the infamous Mars bar), and the month before he left for Canada he appeared at Aylesbury Crown Court for cocaine possession.

As Keith said at the time: 'Being famous is OK but in the courtroom it only counts against you.' Talk about obliging, he had even shown the arresting officer how to operate his cassette recorder before taking a statement. Thankfully he was acquitted and able to travel to Canada.

In the weeks leading up to the trip, Keith grew more and more excited. He is never happier than when the Rolling

Stones are working and once said: 'I can't live without being on the road.' When the touring stopped, when your best friends weren't down the corridor, when the buzz from performing in front of massive, adoring crowds was gone, he eventually struggled and turned to drugs to replace that high. That's how he explains it.

The shows at the El Mocambo (capacity 300) were the first the band had done since playing to 200,000 in England the summer before. Incredibly they were to be the first club shows the band had played since 1964. The idea was to record them for a forthcoming live album. They took place on 4 and 5 March and it is a testament to the band's dedication and stamina that they pulled them off under such trying circumstances. It was bizarre in the extreme, rehearsing all through the night at a large warehouse in a nowhere part of town, then returning to the hotel in the early hours of the morning through a maze of basement corridors to avoid the throng of media and fans camped outside the hotel. It was crazy.

Once the band hit the tiny stage, you would never have known the chaos that surrounded them in the run-up to the shows. The set was an electric combination of blues songs that originally inspired them, including Bo Diddley's 'Cracking Up' (how apt), 'Route 66', Chuck Berry's 'Around and Around' and 'Little Red Roster', coupled with never-before-heard live versions of newer Stones gems: 'Crazy Mama', 'Dance Little Sister' and 'Memory Motel', and the stone-cold classics 'All Down the Line', 'Honky Tonk Women', 'It's Only Rock 'n' Roll' and 'Rip This Joint'.

And that's what they did. They tore the place up. The first night was exceptional but the second night was one of those 'you had to be there' moments. Listening back now to the unmixed, straight-off-the-monitor tapes, it was sensational. Keith particularly was on fire, playing one out-of-this-world guitar solo after another. Outside it was freezing but inside it was so hot the beer would be lukewarm by the time you took a second sip. Sweat poured from every audience member, full of mostly radio competition winners, along with Margaret Trudeau, wife of the then Canadian Prime Minister Pierre Trudeau, whose appearance at the shows grabbed even more global headlines, somehow managing to knock Keith off quite a few front pages.

By the time Monday dawned, the grim reality of the situation hovered like a very dark cloud. Keith and Anita appeared in court. Anita was fined and Keith was given bail, his passport confiscated. They returned to their home for the foreseeable future, the thirty-second floor of the Harbour Castle Hotel. Outside Lake Ontario was frozen. It would melt by the time they left. A life of quite decent Valpolicella and room service cheeseburgers beckoned.

The future for Keith and indeed the Rolling Stones was uncertain. A couple of days after the court appearance Mick Jagger flew to New York City and soon after the others followed. Within days the Stones party of forty-eight had dwindled to just ten. I was moved to the suite next door to Keith, Anita and Marlon. I'm sure Keith felt alone and quite possibly betrayed but no doubt my staying helped forge a tremendous bond between us. It also provided upfront and personal insight into the man I was writing a book about and a treasure trove of colour.

God knows what my parents thought. I called home frequently, as I always did, and constantly reassured them I was fine, but it must have been a massive worry, knowing their loving daughter was living for a month in a Toronto hotel alongside a Rolling Stone out on bail for heroin trafficking.

It's going to be a really great book, I promised them.

The first couple of days after the shows, Keith stayed in except for court appearances, listening again and again to the live tapes interspersed with Dylan's classic *Blood on the Tracks*. Among the more cherished things Keith often gave friends were cassettes, mixtapes of music he loved and often tracks he played on, personally titled and with lovingly written inlay cards. The Mocambo live tapes were appropriately dubbed 'The Cockroaches', which was how Keith referred to the band sometimes.

Later in the week, fed up with a steady diet of room service and old movies, Keith took Marlon to Toronto's biggest department store, Eaton's, and bought him some toys. He also visited the record department (those were the days) and bought some old Elvis Presley *Sun Sessions* albums and a big stack of blank cassettes. Walking round a department store in the middle of the day with Keith Richards was a hard one to fathom but it was really happening. It was the new reality for this Rolling Stone right then.

A few kids approached with a thumbs up while a crop of 'Keef Is Innocent' T-shirts and badges surfaced round the world. When Keith finally got back to his day job and returned to Stones action, he had guitar picks made that read: 'I'm Innocent'. And when the band recorded *Some Girls* in Paris later that year, he wrote the classic 'Before They Make Me Run' about his troubles with the law.

The one time the family strayed further than Toronto was for a day outing to the Canadian side of Niagara Falls – prompting Keith to quip: 'Shall I jump?' – before returning to the prison-like confines of the hotel. It made a nice change for us all.

For a long time Keith's public persona revolved around his personification of cool and his bad-boy behaviour. Few would know how funny he is, possessing that classic dry British humour. At the time he was a big fan of Monty Python and the Derek and Clive tapes made by Peter Cook and Dudley Moore, infamous for a sketch about Jayne Mansfield and a lobster. Use your imagination! He'd listen to them for hours and also spent a great deal of time reading, and still does – mostly history books. But music of course was his main love.

A week after the first club show Keith booked some studio time, initially to listen to the live tapes but once there he started to record some incredibly moving versions of mostly country classics, the ache in his voice heartbreaking. The young studio engineers were in awe, as stunned as the people at Eaton's. All-round Stones crony and master of the boogie-woogie piano, Ian Stewart, stayed behind to look after all things Keith, and he added his piano prowess to some of the tracks.

These Toronto sessions showcased a musical side to Keith that hadn't been exposed much before, or since, save for the occasional track on Stones albums, but there is so much more to him than the guitar anchor and song maestro that makes the Stones tick. Here he is, alone in the studio, playing piano on most of the downbeat songs and a bit of acoustic guitar, singing in a plaintive voice that could easily reduce one to tears, knowing his current predicament. If Keith ever made a solo album, this is what it could sound like. This is music he learnt from his friend, the late, great Gram Parsons (check out early Flying Burrito Brothers, Emmylou Harris's first album and solo work). Gram also hung out when the Stones made their classic *Exile on Main Street* in the South of France. You can hear his influence as well on the track 'Country Honk' from *Let It Bleed*.

Keith turned me on to lots of great reggae too, another of his passions. Max Romeo, Toots and the Maytals, obviously

Bob Marley. Through Keith, I also got hip to zydeco, a French country Cajun music, and the wonderful Clifton Chenier. The songs he recorded in Toronto opened me up to a new world of country music and I found myself becoming a big fan quite quickly. The music had an emotional pull that was hard to resist: George Jones, Merle Haggard, Tammy Wynette. Keith ripped into Tammy's 'Apartment #9', Merle Haggard's 'Sing Me Back Home', George Jones's 'Say It's Not You' and the blues standard 'Worried Life Blues'. Lyrically and musically all the songs touched a chord in Keith and took the breath away from everyone in the room. They were stunning, emotional, painful, honest and real. Everything music should be and so often isn't. He spent many nights in that month of March 1977 in the studio creating magic. And in his hotel room listening back to it.

I will forever cherish the cassettes he gave me from those sessions, personally addressed 'To Barbara', with an asterisk which noted 'just piano and vocal, no overdubs' for some tracks. Even on these cassettes for friends, he was always the professional.

Previous tapes he gave me were titled 'Vinyl Solution' with one side 'Vinyl Affair', another 'A Bit of Old Tongue' complete with the Stones logo as drawn rather well by Keith and one inscribed 'Happy New Year from the Walking Wounded', another 'Flagging Strolling Bones', all personally signed.

In a weird hazy way the month sped by and on 1 April Keith's passport was returned and he was granted a US visa on medical grounds and allowed to travel to the States for rehab. I was still on the *Sounds* payroll and needed to file some stories so I hightailed it to New Orleans to cover Genesis on tour, now without lead singer Peter Gabriel.

I flew to New Orleans and then Dallas and hit the ground

running. It was a great way to mark my re-entry into the real world as I was quite friendly with Genesis and they greeted me warmly, curious to hear of my Canadian adventures. I felt like I was returning to earth from the moon and to say I over-did it the first night is no understatement. The combination of the live show, new surroundings, new people and various substances made it hard for me to get out of bed the next morning to fly to Dallas for the second Genesis show that I was covering for *Sounds*. I was so hung-over I missed my flight. I'll never forget the awful humidity in New Orleans, the hotel front desk constantly ringing, at first asking me to vacate the room, then demanding it and eventually banging on the door, all while my head was pounding. That's what a month in Toronto will do. Imagine how Keith felt! I have to admit, by this point in the story that I was no stranger to the rock 'n' roll life, smoking Marlboros like a chimney, drinking Jack Daniel's and smoking plenty of pot, and not averse to the not-so-odd line of cocaine.

I stayed in the US, now freelancing for *Sounds* and other US magazines. It was a bit of a nomadic existence, living in hotels when on assignment all over the States, and when in New York City staying with my sister in her cosy Fifteenth Street apartment, just off Third. I was there in July 1977 when the infamous NYC blackout happened. The entire city just went dark from 9.30 p.m. My sister was understandably worried when she couldn't find me though she eventually discovered me smoking pot with a neighbour on the roof of their building! Money was tight and I vividly remember buying a bottle of red wine for us that same summer, literally with whatever coins I had left, walking back to her apart-ment and somehow the wine fell out of the bottom of the paper bag and smashed. We laughed through tears as I had no money to buy another bottle!

Following a stint in rehab, Keith was now holed up in Cherry Hill, New Jersey, living in the suburbs and eating lots of local diner takeaway. He spent a lot of time listening to the tapes of what would become the *Love You Live* LP with some tracks from the El Mocambo shows. He eventually moved to a rented house in Westchester, Connecticut which was more suitable to his preferences. I visited often.

I filed a lot of stories about the Stones, using interviews that would eventually be in my book, and also while in LA reviewed a wonderfully exciting show by Tom Petty and the Heartbreakers at the Whisky a Go Go, interviewed Linda Ronstadt, Alice Cooper, Warren Zevon and lots of others. I remember staying at the Sunset Marquis that August, sitting by the pool when we heard the news that Elvis Presley had died, which just shocked the whole musical community.

Most of my days were taken up with research for the Keith book; it took a lot of time and perseverance to track down former associates and relatives and convince them to talk to me. Keith was always happy to send a note or speak to them on the phone to reassure them the book had his full approval. The cast of characters I interviewed provided tremendous insight and wonderful stories and included the Stones' absolutely legendary first manager Andrew Loog Oldham, guitar tech Ted Newman Jones, Keith's long-lost dad Bert, his mother Doris, the late, great engineer Andy Johns, his brother Glyn, the producer Jimmy Miller, ex-Stone Mick Taylor, Ian Stewart and of course the band themselves.

The bulk of the band interviews were done in Paris when they were recording what would become *Some Girls* – working title 'More Fast Numbers' – in late 1977 and early '78. Keith stayed at his rue Saint-Honoré flat and I stayed at the Hotel Frontenac, a small five-star hotel off the Champs-Élysées, with Bill Wyman, Charlie Watts and others in the party. It was on rue de Charon, which amused me greatly.

Before Christmas, Keith returned to Toronto and a trial date was set for February '78 though later moved to October. The band were in fine creative form but talk of 'what if Keith goes to prison?' would not stop. The future remained uncertain, which added a massive sense of drama to everything the Stones did.

Keith very graciously let me stay at Redlands, his West Wittering home, to write my book as it had been empty ever since he flew to Toronto. It's a little over a two-hour drive from London, past Guildford, Horsham and just beyond Chichester, near the sea. It's a really beautiful part of England. I spent the first part of 1978 ensconced in the house on my own, transcribing countless cassettes. There's nothing more inspiring than writing about a subject as charismatic as Keith, in his home, and I was one lucky lady. I wrote the book on a manual typewriter as computers didn't exist yet. Being left-handed, any corrections were a nightmare, as the newly applied Tipp-Ex would smudge along the sentence, blurring the whole thing when I tried to make any changes, leaving lovely white spattered spots along my left hand. You read that right, no computers. And no internet. No mobile phones. If you needed to check a fact, you actually had to check it with the source. No instant information.

I'd write all day and at night make dinner, then roll a few joints, have a glass of wine and watch TV, though there was not much to chose from and most nights there was absolutely nothing on. I eventually started watching midweek football (soccer to our US friends) and got hooked. I came back to London before the season ended in 1978 and, as I still lived on Sloane Street, my nearest club was Chelsea. I don't think I went to a game then but later that year I started going, dragging friends who were more interested in getting drunk before the game than the game itself. It remains one of my great passions and pleasures in life.

Some Girls came out in June 1978 and the band toured the US. They spent the first week of October in New York City rehearsing for *Saturday Night Live*, which at the time was the biggest entertainment show in America, introducing a whole new generation of comedians. It got the best and biggest bands to play live and would be the first TV the Stones had done since *The Ed Sullivan Show* way back when. It was quite the occasion.

Rehearsals were total insanity. The *SNL* cast members then included John Belushi and Dan Aykroyd. Suffice to say, there were a lot of late nights. The show aired live from the NBC Radio City studios on 7 October and the after-show lasted well into 8 October. John Belushi had a larger-than-life appetite so it was some celebration.

Two weeks later Keith flew to Toronto for the trial – there was no jury, just a judge –– and stayed at the Four Seasons. I flew up the night before. Crucially, Jane Rose, by now virtually managing Keith, kept the atmosphere calm and we all did our best to remain upbeat. Keith retained his sense of humour throughout but deep down he must have been incredibly scared. On hearing that Sid Vicious had slit his wrists (the week before he'd been charged with killing his girlfriend at New York's Chelsea Hotel), Keith joked: 'He's trying to steal my headlines.'

On the morning of 23 October, nattily dressed in a three-piece rust-coloured suit and shades, Keith left for court. His lawyer presented the case, which took most of the day. When Keith left for court the next day, wearing the same suit, he left jewellery and his prized Cartier lighter behind in the hotel room, just in case he didn't return. By 12.30 he was a free man and the ordeal was over. The prosecution pressed for a six- to twelve-month jail sentence but the judge gave Keith the most unorthodox sentence imaginable. He was ordered to play a concert for the Canadian National Institute for the Blind (a blind fan had testified at the trial) within the next six months. London's *Evening Standard* ran a cartoon with blind people proclaiming: 'What did we do wrong?'

He was also ordered to continue a programme to stay healthy and meet regularly with a probation officer. A press conference was held and afterwards we flew by helicopter to New York City. If I told you Keith Richards went to see Dave Edmunds' Rockpile at the Bottom Line and jumped onstage for two songs the very next night, would you believe me? Of course you would! He was given a hero's welcome by the crowd and by the NYPD who were outside the venue. A new day had dawned and my book had a happy ending.

BC and Rose Charone, NYC

Chapter 5
All That Jazz

For Christmas that year I gave my parents a one-year subscription to the British satirical magazine *Private Eye*. That tells you something about how out of touch I was with reality. I was living on a cloud of Keith Richards and the Rolling Stones and enjoying every minute of it. It was incredibly surreal.

Private Eye is a great read if you live in the UK but if you live anywhere else it literally makes next to no sense at all as it concerns itself exclusively with the British press, British politics and everyday life in the UK. Alarm bells must have rung in the Charone household whenever the new issue arrived, rather belatedly, in the post.

Around this time friends were also not sure if they could call me at 3 a.m. or 3 p.m. In fact my good friend Moira Bellas was so concerned that at one point she threatened to call my parents. She was worried I would submerge myself in a rock 'n' roll lifestyle that wouldn't be good for my mental or physical health.

Despite all the rock 'n' roll carousing I had been taking part in, my relationship with my parents was always great. I got a very small advance for the book as these were just very early days for music biographies and there was no money in it. Keith generously paid for my flight to Toronto and the month-long stay at the Harbour Castle Hotel and my parents helped me out financially whenever necessary.

One of our many bonds was still music and the arts but specifically musicals. *A Chorus Line* had taken Broadway by storm in 1975 and I shared my parents' enthusiasm for this truly innovative, ground-breaking musical. The show broke box-office records and whenever I was in New York City I could not resist a visit to the Shubert Theatre where it ran for years and years. I must have seen it at least fifteen times plus a couple more when it opened in London. We used to play the cast album constantly whenever I visited and even dance around the living room, to paraphrase a line from one of the songs in the show.

Another landmark family moment was the Bob Fosse autobiographical film *All That Jazz* that came out in the summer of 1980. I remember my mother phoning to tell me how fantastic it was, how it made her think of me and how she could not wait to see it with me. And she was as good as her word. The next time I was in Chicago the first thing we did was go see the movie because it really resonated in our household. My dad and sister loved it too, and the soundtrack was permanently on our turntable.

Fosse had directed a lot of classic Broadway shows that my parents saw when visiting New York City. Every time they saw a great show, they bought the cast album and we got to experience it through the music while growing up so I was understandably hooked on musicals. Fosse was particularly famous for his striking 'jazz hands' choreography, often revolving around a top hat and hand movements that just took your breath away. In many ways, *A Chorus Line* was a tribute to the Fosse style, especially in the show's penultimate number 'One' when the entire chorus line breaks out into what could only be described as a Fosse-like dance number.

Two of Fosse's early hits were *The Pajama Game*, about a union lawyer, so obviously there was no way we could resist its charms; and *Damn Yankees*, which my dad particularly loved, about an ageing baseball player who sells his soul to the devil for one more season. A bigger hit was *Chicago*, where his trademark dance moves were the star of the show despite the great score. At Christmas, we'd do exuberant routines around the house to the music from these shows, especially *A Chorus Line*, and even had top hats to go with it. In 2019 the TV series, *Fosse/Verdon*, which documents his career, was a critical hit. Gwen Verdon was a dancer and actress who became Fosse's muse and starred in many of his shows. The acclaimed series stars Sam Rockwell and Michelle Williams and really captures their turbulent relationship.

With my Keith Richards book finished, I now had to get its subject to sign off his approval and to do so he had to read the manuscript. So back to Paris I went, waiting for Keith to read the book. As deadline day dawned, he still hadn't read it, which caused me quite a lot of anxiety. It was both surreal and nerve-racking sitting in the flat while he read the book.

Without his signature, there was no book. The galleys were literally at the printer's, and I worried not just about getting him to OK the book but the very real possibility he could make a lot of changes or indeed ask for whole chapters to be taken out or rewritten.

Once again, Keith did not let me down and, after reading the book, asked simply for two changes to be made: one was a date that was incorrect and the other was about a guitarist who auditioned for Mick Taylor's vacancy but didn't get the job. Keith didn't want to embarrass him.

On 22 April Keith finally did his 'time' by playing two concerts at Toronto's 5,000-capacity Oshawa Auditorium for the Canadian National Institute for the Blind. The excitement in the hall was palpable and backstage the atmosphere was insane. Jane Rose orchestrated the whole thing. *SNL* cronies Dan Aykroyd, John Belushi and director Lorne Michael mingled with friends and family. The first half of the show was Ron Wood's band, the New Barbarians (Keith had played on Ron's excellent first solo outing *I've Got My Own Album to Do*). The second half of the show was the Stones. The place went mental and it was surreal walking round the hall full of adoring blind fans. Understandably the merchandise was in Braille and I still have the sweatshirt Keith signed for me in dots.

My book, simply titled *Keith Richards*, was published in the UK that September. I was beyond excited and loved doing interviews for radio and print. However, no sooner was the book in print than the publisher Futura was bought by McDonald, who specialised in educational books, becoming McDonald Futura. And while my book was indeed educational for those of a rock 'n' roll persuasion, it was not what the new company had signed up for, so the chances of my book even being in most bookstores were suddenly remote. Very bad luck.

I fared better in the US where Doubleday picked it up. I wrote an additional chapter and in 1982 it came out with a new jacket and a new title: *Life As a Rolling Stone*. The book was also published in Germany and in Japan, where Mick Jagger was on the front cover and Keith on the back. At first I was appalled before someone explained that's how the Japanese language works, back to front!

I'd been living in the UK since 1974 on a work permit which was renewable each year. *Sounds* had originally sorted it out for me, and when I left I continued to be eligible for it as I was a writer. As an American, I had a unique perspective which suited the criteria. After five years of working legally in the UK you could apply for permanent residency, which I did. I was quietly confident of getting this status but also filled with worry in case I didn't, as London was clearly my home and to have to leave would have been devastating.

The day the letter from the Home Office arrived granting me permanent residency was a day worth celebrating, although no different from most days for me as I was at something of a loose end. Writing a book had been a major career goal and now it was over. I'd spent the best part of three years writing about someone else's life, an incredibly interesting one at that, but now I felt a bit like Keith must feel when the touring stops: parachuted back into the real world and not really sure which direction to take.

I spent a lot of time enjoying being back full-time in London and would come home, often from long nights and sometimes early mornings with friends, and lay on the floor of my massive one-room flat, and listen to *Beggars Banquet* or *Let It Bleed* or *Exile on Main Street* on very big, fabulous headphones. Clearly, I wasn't quite ready to let go.

The flat was part of what must have once been an old townhouse on Sloane Street that was now divided into flats. It faced the street, had very high ceilings, two big windows, a large windowless kitchen and a rather small bathroom. I had a fantastic stereo and did a fair bit of entertaining. There were many nights when a bunch of us would come back to mine after dinners out or after a show and stay late into the night playing music, talking like mad as the cocaine took hold of our senses. I remember all too well spilling one of those little packets on the floor one time and all of us furiously trying to scrape it off the maroon carpet.

Luckily I still had access to Cadogan Gardens. Lots of similar private gardens are dotted all over London, especially in Kensington, Chelsea and Notting Hill. They are very

English and something you'll often see in movies. Check out Julia Roberts and Hugh Grant in *Notting Hill* and you'll get an idea of how lovely, quaint and so very English they are. This particular garden had two tennis courts, which enabled me to get a bit of physical exercise.

Having spent three years in the dream world of the Rolling Stones, I returned to London and thought nothing of spending £50 on a gram of cocaine. No wonder I had a big overdraft! Some mornings, having been up all night, still wired and with nothing to watch across the three channels (Channel 4 would not start till late 1982), I'd drive into the West End, go to one of the massive record stores and for the very princely sum of something close to £50, buy a video to watch. My perspective on the value of money had obviously all but disappeared.

I had always loved tennis, and used to watch my dad play on Saturday mornings before taking up the game myself. In those days you could roll up in the Wimbledon car park, across the street from the club, and buy a ticket for that day's match from one of the many touts. As the matches got closer and closer to the final of the tournament, the price rose but for the same £50 you could go to the men's final. A bargain! The quality of tennis in the late seventies and early eighties was fantastic and there were an awful lot of personalities in the game. That summer of 1980 I went to most of the key matches including the final between John McEnroe and Björn Borg, probably the best tennis match ever played. Borg won the five-set thriller, which included a fourth-set tie break McEnroe won 18–16, having saved numerous match points.

Unfortunately my ticket was way up the back of Centre Court, next to a man the size of two seats and that, coupled with the heat, the many glasses of champagne before the match and the length of the final (five hours), caused me to drop off a few times. I was back the following year, when McEnroe won, and managed to stay awake throughout the match! John was something of a rock star himself and celebrated accordingly after the final. Instead of going to the Champions' Ball he hung out with the Pretenders.

My parents frequently visited London during the Wimbledon fortnight and my dad and I would go to the matches. By now I had graduated to applying for tickets in the public draw, in my own and all my friends' names, and their pets' names, and always had tickets for the men's quarters, semis and final. I've been to the Wimbledon final every year since 1980 until 2020 when the tournament was cancelled due to the pandemic. My dad passed away in 1993, but I can never go to Wimbledon or even watch it on TV without thinking of him. Back then there was no roof over Centre Court, so when it rained, which it did often, there was no play. Entire days' play were cancelled due to the rain, so you would drink Pimm's with only your umbrella for cover, listening to the tournament director saying he would update us in an hour, that play might start in a few hours. I had the misfortune to be there the day Cliff Richard 'entertained' Centre Court by singing. Somehow the rain was part of the fun. Those were great days and cherished times.

Years later I was at a Wimbledon final with my friend Keith Blackmore, who was then deputy editor of *The Times*. We were sitting next to film director Sam Mendes and his son. At some point after the first set, Sam asked if either of us had any cash he could borrow as he was meeting his son and wanted to buy a drink. Keith didn't but I happily gave him £20. And that was the last I ever saw of it.

In the early days, I often drove to Wimbledon in my second-hand Datsun, which was a rather garish shade of blue. I'd bought it from Emerson, Lake & Palmer's manager

Stuart Young. Don't worry, it wasn't *his* car – he'd bought it for his girlfriend. He had a much nicer car. Much like my first car, the bright orange Mini Metro, you could see this Datsun clearly wherever you parked it, which was a big advantage in the enormous Wimbledon car park. No doubt there were night I should not have driven. These were the days when Quaaludes were popular, a sort of sleeping pill that for some reason people took to get high, although I think low would be a better description. One night I'd had a few and for some reason was in the Datsun, driving down Piccadilly past the Ritz, obviously on my way home to Sloane Street, and inadvertently bumped along some railings more than once, adding to the Datsun's rather lived-in look. Eventually I sold the car for £50, its scrap-metal price.

Obviously, I couldn't carry on like that forever. I went to see quite a few gigs, mostly club shows of new post-punk bands including the Boomtown Rats and the Pretenders, a great band led by the inimitable Chrissie Hynde. They were just starting to happen and we became friends. They'd been in the flat, as had Genesis, when Phil Collins's first wife got stuck in the bathroom (jammy lock).

Having written the book, I didn't really want to go back to the daily routine of life as a rock critic. In the three-plus years I had been at *Sounds* I had written an awful lot of articles, live reviews, record reviews, thousands and thousands of words every week. Writing a book had been a challenge and creatively very rewarding. Consequently I felt that chapter of my career was now over. I started to freelance for the *Daily Mail*, a popular national newspaper that pretended to be *The Times* but was really the *Sun*, though not as good. It was an interesting experience to write for a national newspaper about music. These were the early days of music journalism even appearing in daily papers. Some of the articles I wrote appeared exactly as I wrote them and some were edited into something I hardly recognised. The last straw was that, according to the studio, they sent a reporter to the Stones' studio in Paris saying I had said it was OK for them to come in. As if that would ever happen. I was furious with the paper and rang the showbiz editor to complain. It was a good lesson for what would be my future career, but I didn't know that yet.

Thatcher had been elected prime minister and it was quite a bleak period for the UK. The IRA were carrying out bombings in the country quite regularly and for a long time I would always avoid walking past those iconic red post boxes as they had been known to blow up and cause serious injury to anyone nearby. Once I was at a show at Wembley Arena and was positive the guy behind me had a bomb because he had a package in a paper bag he kept looking at throughout the show. Eventually I discovered he was taping the show on a cassette machine and was afraid of being caught.

Another time I was coming back from Stamford Bridge, where Chelsea play at the end of the Fulham Road, and there were hundreds of people spilling out onto the streets around my flat. It transpired that a bomb had gone off in a car right near Harrods and the entire store and whole area had been evacuated. Scary times indeed.

Aside from going to shows, I pursued my growing fascination with football and went regularly to Chelsea, eventually getting a season ticket. The first four years I lived in the UK I knew nothing about football but once I did, I embraced it passionately. Football takes up so much of the national conversation and occupies so much space in the papers and daily life that I really don't know what I'd do without it. As a football fan living in the UK, you can spend any taxi journey, no matter how long, happily chatting about the sport and arguing about which team is best, yours or his.

Fed up with dragging half-interested, half-inebriated friends to a game, I was delighted when a friend suggested I meet one of their friends, who was looking for someone to go to Chelsea with. That person was Paul Conroy. At the time he worked for Stiff Records, which was enjoying massive success with Elvis Costello, Nick Lowe and Madness, to name but three. His dad was now too old to go to games so we developed a wonderful football-based friendship which is still going strong today, though he doesn't go to the matches any more. We would later work together.

At some point early in 1981 Moira suggested I take a job working for her in the press department at WEA Records. Their office was on Broadwick Street in Soho, round the corner from Carnaby Street, quite a hub for publishing and music. It was also around the corner from the infamous Marquee Club on Wardour Street where so many amazing bands got their start.

My job as staff writer was to write original press releases on albums, singles and tours for UK artists and bands on the label and edit all the American press releases on the US acts into something that worked here. I did all this once again on a manual typewriter, as computers had still not been invented. Sales of Tipp-Ex rose dramatically.

I joined WEA on £8,000 a year and I owed the bank £10,000. In the time spent finishing the book and starting the job, I had accrued quite a bit of debt. At one point I thought I would sue Barclays Bank for letting me get such a big overdraft. As I said earlier, I was very good at talking people into things, very convincing, and each time I needed more funds, my bank manager agreed.

Without a doubt, I needed to cut down my expenses and say goodbye to the high life. I stopped smoking cigarettes, stopped taking coke (except occasionally when someone else offered), stopped smoking pot and started to live like a grown-up. I kept the Chelsea season ticket – it was only £250 then(!) – and moved forward into a new career, still working in music, and happy to embrace routine once again.

After a year or so, someone in the press office left and Moira asked if I wanted to be a press officer. It seemed like a good idea, especially as I had been a journalist so I knew very well what I'd be dealing with. One of the first acts I had to work on was a solo effort from the Modern Romance singer Geoff Deane. Modern Romance were a popular novelty group, best known for their hits 'Everybody Salsa' and a cover of 'Cherry Pink and Apple Blossom White' – I kid you not.

We had weekly press meetings with the team of eight people where we talked about what was achieved, what needed to be achieved and what was lacking for each of the current acts on the roster. When it came to Geoff Deane, Moira asked if I had called the *NME* to see if they would write about him. Of course I hadn't. I was too embarrassed. Moira explained rather succinctly that I better make that call or this wasn't going to work out. As someone else now had my old job, there was no going back. It was a big lesson learnt.

The second act I got to work on was a bit more exciting than Geoff Deane. A young US artist from Detroit. Her name was Madonna. And once again, my life would never be the same.

BC in photo pit at Castle Donington festival,
mid 1980s

Chapter 6
Lucky Star

Working in an office was just what I needed. And working at one of the major record companies seemed the perfect bookend to my already successful career in the music business. Being a publicist felt as natural as crossing the road; I was just on the other side and it suited me down to the ground. My strength had always been communication, enthusiasm and my total love of music. Having been a journalist, I had the natural advantage of being able to know where to position an artist in a paper, how to pitch, what a story entailed, and other assets including the mechanics of the actual interview.

You'd be surprised how many novice PRs, and sometimes not so novice, think, Yes, please, when the *Sunday Times* or the *Guardian* ring up and want to interview one of your clients. But you always have to ask yourself why. Ditto the tabloid end. All press isn't necessarily good press, especially in a country like the UK that has so much of it. Quality not quantity is the byword.

Some basic tips: don't do the interview in a noisy place. Try not to do it with more than two members of a band as they all talk over each other and if there's any more the writer won't be able to decipher who said what when they transcribe the tape. Don't let the manager or the US PR sit in on the interview; it's hard enough to get a sense of someone without being watched or judged. Make sure the artist knows the writer's name. There's nothing more impressive to a writer than the artist actually calling you by your name, and when it's a massive star like Mick Jagger you're often reduced to the status of a very grateful fan.

WEA was on the up and a new chairman had just been appointed. He was having a tour of the building and meeting staff when he walked into the press office. Michael Jackson's 'Beat It' was on the stereo. I was standing on a desk, playing air guitar to the Eddie Van Halen guitar solo that drove the tune. Hello, Mr Chairman, and welcome to the jungle otherwise known and loved as the press department. Artists often congregated within our comfy surroundings.

We were the least corporate department in the company with the exception of A & R, the mostly men who signed the artists. We were the fans who almost grew up, got lucky and were able to make a career in music. I was still in the glorious position of being paid to listen to music all day. Who wouldn't love that?

Our office was deep in the heart of Soho and luckily for us *Smash Hits* and *NME* were both based on Carnaby Street, just around the corner. The two titles were polar opposites and neatly encapsulated almost everything you needed for a good PR campaign. *NME* was drinking in the rarefied air of being the most credible music paper in the country, with massive sales, while new kid on the block *Smash Hits* had discovered pop in all its glory and thrived on asking artists deep and meaningful questions like: 'What colour is Wednesday?' Some artists embraced the fun while others were nervous. What was the right answer? There is no right answer!

Smash Hits was in glorious widescreen and Technicolor, everything in its pages as bright as anything Boy George wore in those early days of Culture Club. It embraced anything with a pop pulse and the world was all the better for it. It was run by the charts and by what was popular, whereas *NME* was run by what was cool. The colour pages of *Smash Hits* were quite a contrast to the mostly black-and-white spreads in *NME*, *Melody Maker* and *Sounds*.

We were lucky enough to have a TV in Moira's office so every Thursday several *Smash Hits* staff members would come by and watch *Top of the Pops*, the weekly chart rundown show which was essential viewing for anyone working in the music business. We'd open a bottle of wine and a bag of crisps and off we'd go talking up or down everyone on the show with much hilarity, a little bit of bitchiness but a lot of fun.

One of those staff members was Neil Tennant, later the singer in the Pet Shop Boys, who almost forty years later remains a very good friend. *Smash Hits* writers would also come by our office to watch any videos they were sent by other labels, allowing us to build really good working relationships with them. We were able to get their attention and pitch our artists. We didn't have to wait for them to call us back. We could also show them videos of our new artists that we wanted them to champion after they watched whatever they had come in with on one of those big black VHS tapes.

As their circulation rose, so did the coverage of our artists in their hallowed pages. A *Smash Hits* cover was as cherished by the marketing department as an *NME* cover – it just depended what suited the artist in question. A bit like the *Sun* or the *Guardian*. It's a particular skill to know who fits where and as I was and still am a total newspaper junkie, I was good at it. The ideal artist fits everywhere.

Music was starting to occupy more and more space in the papers as they began to dip their collective toes into the murky waters of the pop world. The tabloids and the London *Evening Standard* soon all had pop columns but the broadsheets took a bit longer to read the temperature and gauge where music fit into their landscape. These days it is not unusual to have an artist's interview trailed above the masthead on the *Guardian* or *The Times* or the *Telegraph* but back then it was inconceivable.

Smash Hits also had no access to the midweek charts – which helped them decide what acts to cover in their fortnightly magazine – so they would call me for the midweeks which the record company received. Midweeks were a prediction of where the song would be in the top 40 chart, based on their midweek sales. They would also then call me for the final chart positions. These days the press have access to chart positions during the week but back then we held the magic cards.

It was great giving them the chart positions and bigging up our artists. It really helped develop long-standing social relationships with the writers. Obviously, I used a bit of poetic licence with our artists and wasn't averse to telling them the single midweek was up even if it was down. No harm in that! After all, I wanted a feature in *Smash Hits*. I always saw it, and still do, as a competition. There's a very competitive element to doing press, in being a PR, driven by a desire to win, to convince, persuade, to secure the cover. It's totally addictive and when the results go your way, very satisfying. When they don't, very frustrating.

You were the hero if you got a cover or a big feature. And the pressure was on to achieve these results with all the priority acts. Not every project had a happy ending. There were times when I failed and did not secure the cover or, worse still, the feature or review was negative. But mostly my results were very positive and drove me on to glory.

One of the very first acts I had to use a bit of coercion with was Madonna. Her first two singles, 'Everybody' in 1982 and 'Burning Up' in 1983, didn't chart but helped create a nice buzz.

Her manager at the time (Freddy DeMann, who also managed Michael Jackson) was very underwhelmed with what the label were doing on her behalf and we almost lost her to another major record company. However, Seymour Stein, who had signed her to his Sire Records label which went through WEA, persevered with us and the rest would very soon be history.

It was third time lucky for Madonna with 'Holiday' in 1983. She was spending quite a bit of time in the UK, playing a few short club sets at the Beat Route club on Greek Street, around the corner from our offices. She was accompanied by two dancers and mimed her way through a couple of tracks. Things started building considerably by the time she played the Camden Palace in October of that year. Her twenty-minute set consisted of those first three singles and the look was eye-catching: crucifix earrings, black top, black skirt, leggings, that hair, the lipstick, the birthmark, the bare navel, the midriff, the whole nine yards. She was electric and danced like Bob Fosse himself was pulling the strings.

We went backstage after the set and, as you often do in this job, told the artist how good it was. In this case, it really was very, very good. 'Really?' Madonna said. We had to reassure her that it was truly very special and that the audience loved it, and indeed they did. Since then I've gone backstage hundreds of times to reassure or give artists well deserved praise after a show. If the show isn't up to scratch, I avoid talking about it at all costs. It's amazing to think that back then even Madonna was in need of a little bit of reassurance too, just like anyone else.

You'd be surprised how many record company executives miss most of a show, go backstage after and tell the artist how great a certain song was only for the artist to look perplexed, explaining that they didn't play that song that night. Not a good look.

I kept the guest list of those writers who came to the Camden Palace and the ones who said they would come but didn't. When Madonna next played London, four years later in 1987, the venue was Wembley Stadium. She's the only artist in history who went from playing to a crowd of just under a thousand people to almost 100,000. Nothing in between. No Shepherd's Bush Empire, no Brixton Academy, no Royal Albert Hall, Town & Country Club, Astoria or even Wembley Arena. Just straight to two nights at Wembley Stadium. No one will ever replicate that achievement.

When she returned to our shores that summer of 1987, she was the biggest star on the planet and every paper and magazine in the country wanted to put her on the front cover. I remember being at Sunday lunch with some friends and one of them wondered how *Time Out*, a popular weekly London listings magazine, had printed as part of their cover story a list of established music journalists who didn't turn up for Madonna's Camden Palace show. The list included one of them. 'How did they know that?' they asked me. 'No idea,' I said. 'Please pass the wine.'

Just before that Camden Palace show, we'd had our first full day of press. I picked Madonna up in a minicab at her bed and breakfast hotel on Queen's Gate, round the corner from the Royal Albert Hall. I had to convince some of the papers to speak to her and assured them if the single 'Holiday' wasn't a hit they didn't have to run the story. Despite the fact that we were running a bit late for our first stop, a photo shoot, she insisted on stopping at the very trendy Kensington Market, a collection of boutiques housed within one massive space on Kensington High Street, to get some shoes. Before I could protest, she jumped out of the car and ran into the market. I had no choice but to follow. She got some shoes and we eventually arrived at the shoot.

Looking back now at those early press schedules, it's heart-warming to see that, like everyone else, Madonna put in the long hours of promo work early on. She had dinner with a writer from *No. 1*, a magazine in the same pop vein as *Smash Hits*, and a photo shoot, had a drink over lunch with *Sounds*, chatted to both *Melody Maker* and *NME* and let them both take photos. She even did *Chartbeat* and *Girl About Town*, which were lower down the food chain. From the start, Madonna grasped the value of publicity and I suspect even in those early days realised she wouldn't have to do all this promo for much longer. She saw where this was going.

People always ask me if Madonna has changed and the simple answer is no. Even back in those heady holidays, she knew what she wanted. She was whip-smart, interested in all the arts, outspoken, opinionated and outwardly very confident. She had an aura about her from the very beginning that just radiated an energy that would not be swept aside. She had buckets of belief and gave off the air of someone who would not be messed about.

We did the press, the single was a hit and she returned early in 1984 to appear on *The Tube*, the wildly popular Friday teatime Channel 4 music show, usually filmed in Newcastle but on this occasion filmed live from the Haçienda in Manchester. Her press itinerary that January was similar to our first round of interviews in October, with the pop magazines even more interested now, and covers started to happen. She did a photo shoot with the *Daily Star*, and for years after those photos would be trotted out again and again to the point where it drove her crazy. I begged the photographer to stop using the shots but for years, every time she came to the UK, those pictures would appear in the papers. The photographer must have bought a mansion on the royalties. Not surprisingly, that early press trip was the only time she ever did photos for the UK press. From that point on, we supplied all the photos. She took control.

Looking back now at her contribution to *NME*'s weekly feature, 'Portrait of the Artist as a Consumer', is both amusing and illuminating. Even then she had a complete sense of who and what she was. And that really hasn't changed. For favourite TV programmes she wrote: 'Yuk – never watch TV!' For other categories she added painter Tamara de Lempicka, for books and reading matter she listed Alice Walker's *The Color Purple*, Milan Kundera and *People* magazine! Not surprisingly, one of her favourite films was *Gentlemen Prefer Blondes*. None of these were typical artist answers.

The Tube was everything *Top of the Pops* wasn't and became an instant hit. Where *TOTP* was uniform and structured, *The Tube* was chaotic, a little bit anarchic and exciting. No one knew what to expect from one show to the next and there was that attractive sense that at any time everything could fall apart. It was essential viewing and like nothing that had been on television before (or since). For years we would open a bottle of wine at 5 p.m. on a Friday and watch the show in the office, staying till it ended at 7 p.m. Madonna did 'Burning Up' and 'Holiday' on the show with two backing dancers. The storm was just beginning to erupt and soon all hell would break loose around the world.

Her debut LP, *Madonna*, came out in summer 1983 and her second album, *Like a Virgin*, was due to come in spring '84. I had sent advance copies of the album to long-lead press so they could review when it came out as their deadlines were weeks if not months before release. The disc however got moved to November to catch up with the US success of 'Holiday' so I had to get them to hold their reviews for another issue. After *The Tube* appearance Madonna spent a lot of time in the US and didn't really return to the UK till summer 1987.

Once again lady luck dealt me a good hand. I was lucky I met Al Rudis in Chicago at a show and lucky he told me to send him some story ideas. I was lucky my parents took us to Europe, lucky I got into a university programme for my junior year in London and lucky to get a full-time job on *Sounds* when I graduated. I was lucky to get to know Keith Richards. Lucky to get to work with Madonna. I've never really had to look for work – one job has effortlessly merged into another throughout my whole career.

And, as luck would have it, the building I lived in on Sloane Street was being renovated and I was offered £8,000 to leave. In those days, £8k was a small fortune and that sum, coupled with some money my dad gave me, enabled me to buy my first flat, in Maida Vale. Moira lived in Maida Vale as did a few other friends and it was a really lovely, up-and-coming area. The flat I liked best backed onto a huge private communal garden and there was a lot of space. The street was really wide and unlike Chelsea this felt more like living in the country within the city. I had seen three flats in the space of an hour, loved one of them and put in an offer. The owner was desperate to sell, and before you could say lucky star, I was living in the first flat that I owned and very happy too.

It wasn't just 'Borderline', 'Material Girl' and 'Into the Groove' for me. I had to work a lot of the hard rock acts on the label too. Mötley Crüe started one day of press at the Café Pacifico, a popular Mexican restaurant in Covent Garden, at 11 a.m. with a round of tequila shots that never stopped. As Atlantic Records were part of WEA, we always had the first band on the bill at the annual Donnington day-long heavy metal music fest, and the headliners. As much of their roster included rock bands, one year Twisted Sister opened and AC/DC closed the show. Or ZZ Top another. The list was endless. And they were mostly all on our label. It was exhausting.

Being at the time the least experienced PR in the press office, I had to go on the coach the label provided for the press that left London early in the morning and returned from the festival site in the Midlands very late. We laid on coffee and doughnuts but most of them were chowing down on sulphate, that very unattractive drug commonly known as speed or the poor man's cocaine. It was one way of staying up all day, I suppose!

Years later when Guns N' Roses were starting out, they came to London and lived in serviced apartments just off Kensington High Street. They played two blistering nights at the legendary Marquee Club on Wardour Street. They were incredibly exciting and very loud. Their frontman Axl Rose was a whirling dervish of adrenaline. It was obvious they were going to be massive and the pressure was on to deliver good press. Despite what you've read about them since, they were gentlemen, and sent me a dozen red roses as a thank you when they left the country. When their debut album, *Appetite for Destruction*, eventually came out, I was touched to see I had a thank you on it even though they spelt my name wrong: Barbara Sharone. Still, over thirty million people have an album with my name on it.

A couple of years later my mobile rang late one night. It was the security guard at the office asking if I knew a particular person whose name they gave me. I was informed that this employee was trying to leave the building with a gold Guns N' Roses disc and they were about to call the police. I pleaded with him not to and thankfully he agreed. This person had been to a gig, had a few too many, come back to the office and for some inexplicable reason taken the disc.

Going back to the office late after a gig was not unusual. Sometimes, high on adrenaline, among other things, with nowhere to go and all the pubs shut, we'd return to our Kensington Church Street office (having moved from Soho) to continue the party as no one wanted to go home. One particularly memorable night, music critic John Harris (now an esteemed political writer at the *Guardian*) and his then girlfriend and now wife, PR Ginny Luckhurst, and a few others came back to my office. We opened some wine and played Rod Stewart records really loud for hours on end. The next morning, when my PA arrived, the office was in total disarray, with empty bottles, ashtrays overflowing (you could smoke then!) and all sorts of mess. I arrived just before 10.30 or what used to be known as Egg McMuffin hour. Always the best hangover cure.

I'd read about this movie *Spinal Tap*, a Christopher Guest parody about a fictional band that was coming out, and arranged to go to a screening before its release in 1984. Having worked with so many rock bands similar to the one so realistically portrayed in Spinal Tap, I could not contain my laughter during the screening and laughed so much the film PR asked if I could attend every screening. It really captures some of the many absurdities of what we all do and to this day is still extremely funny. The scene in the record store when the band do a PA (public appearance) and no one comes is a classic. We've all felt like the local rep in the film who tells the band: 'Go on, kick my ass.' I've felt like that many a time when we've had a press reception for a less than stellar artist, so grateful to see anyone walk through the door, worried no one would.

Neil Tennant worked his way up the *Smash Hits* ladder just as I worked my way up the hierarchy of the WEA press office. We initially bonded over literally eating into my WEA expense account lunch or dinners, watching *Top of the Pops* in Moira's office, going to see bands (New Order a highlight) and playing Rock 'n' Roll Trivial Pursuit in which I had the distinction of being an answer to a question regarding my Keith Richards book!

But we really bonded over a mutual appreciation of the theatre. Prior to meeting Neil, I pretty much went alone if something in the West End took my fancy. We were both big Stephen Sondheim fans and whenever possible went to see all the London productions of his shows, from *Follies* with Dianna Rigg in 1988 to the revival of *A Little Night Music* with Judi Dench; the lovely National production of *Sunday in the Park with George* – a show we both liked but wondered 'what the fuck is this about?'; *Company*; *Sweeney Todd* – the list is endless and the fun we had was boundless. It was great to have someone to share the theatre with.

Occasionally, if we didn't like a play, we'd flip a coin at the interval to see if we'd stay for the second half. Sometimes we'd stay just for the interval drinks as we'd already paid for them. And sometimes we'd both admit to spending much of the first act thinking about what to have for dinner afterwards.

Neil eventually left *Smash Hits* in 1985 to try his luck at being a pop star. Most of his *Smash Hits* cronies could not believe he turned down the editor's job to make records, assuming not much would come of it. There were farewell drinks in the office followed by a last supper at the Gerrard Street Chinatown staple, the Wong Kei. It was cheap, and more importantly it had a great name. As a leaving present, the staff presented Neil with a framed *Smash Hits* cover with his face on it. A few years later, his face would be on all sorts of magazine covers for real and still is now, over thirty-five years later.

Along with his partner in crime, Chris Lowe, the Pet Shop Boys became one of the biggest and best bands to come out of the UK. All those clever lyrics just prove that journalism is a good springboard. We'd come a long way from the days I took Neil and Chris for dinner at the Gallery Rendezvous on Beak Street (excellent Chinese) on my meagre WEA expenses. Neil has achieved so much in his incredible career but for me, no doubt, the crowning glory was nicknaming me BC. The nickname has stuck since those heady *Smash Hits* days and I will forever remain BC to one and all.

When Madonna triumphantly returned to the UK for three dates on her Who's That Girl Tour, sheer pandemonium erupted nationally. She kicked off the mini tour in Leeds at Roundhay Park followed by the two Wembley Stadium shows in August. Every national paper sent someone to the show in Leeds and the excitement was palpable on the train from London. It seemed like everyone on board was going to the show. Every single TV station, radio station and publication wanted her. The phones in the press office never stopped ringing. It was total bedlam. Everyone wanted a ticket.

She celebrated her birthday with a private party at the Groucho Club on Dean Street in Soho. The entire street and the adjoining Old Compton Street was one massive human barricade, with thousands gathered outside to grab a glimpse and the police trying their best to keep things orderly. My date for the evening was Mr Tennant, now a genuine pop star himself with the massive hits 'West End Girls' and 'It's a Sin' to name but two. It was quite a night.

When Madonna left the UK, I threw a 'That Girl's Gone' party for the staff in my glass-panelled office at one end of the floor. You needed a special AAA ('access all areas') laminate I had made up, otherwise the security guard who I arranged to guard entry wouldn't let you in. It had been an incredible experience for everyone connected with Madonna at the label. And it wouldn't be the last.

BC and Dad, New Year's Eve, late 1980s

Chapter 7
Crazy for You

My idyllic existence was shattered, rudely interrupted by real life, when my dad got cancer. I flew home, as did my sister, and we were told he might only have six months left. It started with a pain in his shoulder that he thought came from playing tennis but ended up being myeloma (cancer of the blood). He was young, just fifty-eight years old. Luckily for all of us, he had another, mostly good, mostly healthy ten years left and until the end was largely unaffected except when recovering from chemo treatments. I remember my parents' last visit to London. We went to see the Gershwin musical *Crazy for You* and my dad danced his way out of the theatre.

For me, this was a time of change on many levels. Realising my parents were mortal was part of it. Newspapers in the UK were changing too. In 1986 the *Independent* was launched and was a shining beacon of wonderful journalism, especially in its arts coverage throughout the first decade. It's the paper that brought the world Nick Hornby, Andrew Marr, Bridget Jones creator Helen Fielding and the *New Yorker*'s film critic Anthony Lane. The *Independent* fit snugly between the *Guardian* and *The Times*. It was a totally welcome addition to the growing national paper landscape.

It's hard to believe now, in this era of social media, but

newspapers and magazines carried so much weight politically and culturally. Their circulations were enormous. Millions used to read the *Sun*, *Mirror* and *Mail* daily while the broadsheets had incredibly healthy circulations. Even monthly magazines sold well. It was such a big industry that the media became part of the story. Most of the quality papers had weekly media sections where they interviewed key editors and writers as well as discussing in great detail and with a real sense of importance rising and falling circulations, marketing and all the comings and goings that made national papers and magazines tick. Not only was it another era, it now seems like another lifetime.

The *Independent* wasn't the only new kid on the block. And Neil Tennant wasn't the only *Smash Hits* alumnus to go on to bigger and better things. Mark Ellen and Dave Hepworth, both former *Smash Hits* editors, launched an exciting new monthly music magazine called *Q* the same month (October) as the *Indy*, as the *Independent* was affectionately known. *Q* took some of the same irreverent humour that thrived on *Smash Hits* and threw it into the mainstream music culture. It quickly established itself as a UK *Rolling Stone*, only with warmth, humour and personality, setting new standards for quality writing and photography in the process, especially for its first decade. It survived relatively unscathed till the 2020 pandemic sadly killed if off. RIP *Q*.

Where there's success, there are always imitators, and it wasn't long before more monthly music magazines surfaced, the most noteworthy of which were *Select* and *Vox*. The style bible that was *The Face* also covered music of a certain (cool) genre and was incredibly important for certain artists. Both the publisist and the consumer were literally spoilt for choice and it made the job so much more creative and fun.

It really was a golden age for journalism. *Smash Hits*

gave us Chris Heath and the late, great photographer Eric Watson. *Sounds* gave the world Jon Savage. *Select* offered a slew of future stars their first shot at glory, including Alexis Petridis, John Harris, Miranda Sawyer and Caitlin Moran. *NME* had previously made stars of Julie Burchill and Tony Parsons. Most of these writers have gone on to bigger and better things in TV, film and books and are still working today, which just goes to show what an incredibly creative period it was for journalism.

Mark Ellen and Dave Hepworth were also making a name for themselves on the small screen as hosts of *The Old Grey Whistle Test*. I'm not sure we realised it at the time when we all sat watching *Top of the Pops* in the WEA Broadwick Street press office, but there was a lot of talent in that room. *TOGWT* was like a music magazine on TV with in-depth (for TV!) interviews and exclusive live performances. *The Tube* was for hipsters and *TOTP* for pop kids schooled in the charts. It's so sad none of them exist now, though Jools Holland's *Later* is probably a distant BBC relation to *TOGWT*.

I was now head of press at WEA, and soon to be director of publicity while Moira went on to work in A & R and marketing before becoming managing director. It was the end of an era but the beginning of another.

WEA also had a lot of British talent in those days, from Sisters of Mercy and Echo & the Bunnymen to the Jesus and Mary Chain, and later Primal Scream. Geoff Travis, who created Rough Trade, had a label, Blanco y Negro, that initially went through WEA and gave the world Everything but the Girl and a host of other indie talent that sat well on a major roster.

I was lucky once again to have landed at WEA as it quickly became like family to me. The atmosphere in those days at record companies when the industry was thriving was electric, and there was much bonding among staff. There were annual sales conferences where the sales force – labels actually had salesmen in those days, guys who drove around in their Toyotas with a boot full of records – were entertained for a couple of days every year, previewing all the upcoming releases in exotic places like Bournemouth. Everyone drank their body weight in alcohol and quite often had to pull over on the journey home from Bournemouth to let the queasiness pass. For weeks we'd all gossip about who'd got off with who.

My football buddy Paul Conroy had left the trendy independent label Stiff Records and defected to WEA as one of the main directors. They called themselves the Gang of Four and of course were all men. Moira was one of the few women in the entire music industry in an executive position. Publicity, the art department (who primarily dealt with photo shoots, videos, record sleeves) and artist relations (booking hotels, restaurants and party venues) were seen as jobs for the girls. And while my skills as a PR were appreciated, it was nothing like the way the head of radio was fawned over every time he got a playlist, that highly coveted list of records that stations played. Radio 1 ruled at that time (there was no BBC6 Music and Spotify wasn't even invented) and their playlist was essential for an artist to have a hit record.

The press office dealt with national and regional print press and later on, once the internet sprang into life, online press. For a long while, press was really taken for granted by the record company hierarchy. Years later, when radio stations lost listeners and their numbers plummeted, press finally got the long-overdue respect it merited. After all, it was free advertising.

Paul also lived in Maida Vale, and when his marriage broke up, he bought the ground-floor flat in my building. I'll never forget coming home one night and finding a note under my door saying 'Hollins has been sacked'. He was manager of Chelsea at the time and I absolutely hated him.

Paul eventually left both Maida Vale and WEA (moving to Chrysalis and then Virgin) and when he did, I moved from my second-floor flat to the ground floor. The flat was bigger, with higher ceilings and, more importantly, a balcony overlooking the large, private communal garden with an incredibly beautiful view. Only Hyde Park would have bettered it. Buying that flat was one of the best things I ever did and, as I write this book, I am sitting in the very same flat.

Just after moving flats – the move was easy, as I didn't need a van, just the removal men, who carried the contents of the fridge down the stairs – my parents had a terrible car accident while driving back to Chicago from Stratford, Ontario. They would go to Stratford most summers for the Shakespeare festival. My mother was in a coma in ICU and I flew from London to London, a small city in Canada outside Stratford, to be with them. The fact that my ticket literally said from London to London was the only thing that made me laugh for the entire trip.

This was the first serious accident to happen in the family. When I finally arrived in London, Ontario, having changed planes in Toronto, and went to my dad's hotel room, I saw my mother's handbag in the closet. It made me cry. She was never without that handbag and it was as if her ghost was hanging in the closet. At the time there was a really popular US comedy show called *Mary Hartman, Mary Hartman* and that character, like my mom, always carried a handbag – she even slept with it!

My dad was relatively OK, though he had to use a wheelchair for a week after the accident due to various aches and pains. My mom eventually came out of the coma but had to be flown back to Chicago in a special air ambulance. It was the second, awful, real-life event to invade my ridiculously happy day-to-day existence. Thankfully she made a full recovery.

By this time both Madonna and the Pet Shop Boys were growing in stature, albeit on widely different scales. In the summer of 1989 the Pet Shop Boys threw a massive party at a huge warehouse called Westway Studios. I arrived by taxi and was greeted at the door by their then manager, the larger than life Tom Watkins, who asked me if I wanted an E (it was when Ecstasy was all the rage). I decided to take half because I thought it was worth trying and assumed the quality would be good. Next thing I knew it was 5 a.m., light outside (it was summer) and I didn't understand why my taxi wasn't waiting for me!

I was no stranger to hallucinogens as I experimented with them during my last year of high school and the first couple of years of university. It's mad to think back on it now, but I would actually drive to concerts while high. I remember going to see Traffic at the Auditorium Theatre in Chicago and as the orange Mini Metro turned onto the panoramic Lake Shore Drive heading into the city, the high-rise apartment buildings on my right looked like they were exploding. During the actual show, Steve Winwood's guitar looked like it was a multi-coloured haze moving across the stage. During the interval, we went down to the ladies bathroom to smoke a joint. As if I needed to get high(er)! I also vividly remember going into a record shop on another 'trip', and the records were literally coming off the walls saying, 'Buy me, buy me.' I was such a good consumer.

Mostly, though, when my friends and I took pills, I was the sensible one who ended up spending most of the time reassuring the others that it would all be OK and their trip would end soon as their panic set in and often overshadowed what was supposed to be fun. Being the grown-up wasn't really my intention so it was clearly time to move on.

Madonna was racking up the hits round the world, one after another: 'Like a Prayer', 'Express Yourself', 'Vogue', 'Justify My Love' – the list is endless. The Blonde Ambition Tour hit Wembley Stadium in the summer of 1990. BBC Radio 1 were broadcasting the show live and they asked her not to swear. Not one to take kindly to being told what to do, Madonna threw out as many fucks as she could, managing over twenty in quick succession, much to the horror of the head of radio at the label who had told the BBC not to worry. As always, the show was spectacular.

The UK was quickly becoming Madonna's biggest territory. She dominated the album and singles charts. She was the queen of MTV and sat proudly alongside the rest of MTV royalty: Bowie, Prince and Michael Jackson. It's so sad that Madonna is the only one of them still alive.

When Michael Jackson died in 2009, I was at a dinner given by *The Times* in the Writing Room at Lord's Cricket Ground. The editor of *The Times*, James Harding, had invited an incredible group of people who loved cricket to gather before England were to start a big summer of competition. I had developed a passion for cricket a few years before as Paul Conroy had a spare season ticket that I eventually took over. I had always liked baseball and there are similarities but there's no doubting when the weather is good, it's a lovely way to spend a day out. You can drink, eat, chat and watch sport. Who could ask for more. My interest in cricket also coincided with the national team being quite good.

Several former and current England players were present, as was comedian Frank Skinner and Neil Hannon from the Divine Comedy, who had recorded a couple of cricket-themed albums under the Duckworth Lewis moniker that I worked on, along with most of the people who made *The Times* tick. Just before 10 p.m. all our mobiles started making noise, telling us that Michael Jackson had died. No one could believe it but within minutes most of the room cleared and everyone who worked on the paper hightailed it back to the office to rewrite the next day's front page.

There were only a couple of us left, quite dazed by the sudden turn of events. One was the cricketer Graeme Swann, and after a glass or two of wine, we bonded as he is a big music fan. He gave me his email and for the next of couple years we were quite friendly. That would never happen with a footballer or a famous musician, but cricket is still slightly old school, one of its many charms. I'll always remain indebted to him for getting me tickets to the Ashes we won at the Oval.

I met a lot of interesting characters working with Madonna but the absolute best was her US PR Liz Rosenberg. She is a PR genius, incredibly funny and can write the shit out of a press release. She doesn't panic in a crisis and her gut reaction is usually correct. She has total confidence in herself, which in this job is essential. Like me, she met Madonna in 1983 when she was unknown. We didn't start working together closely until Madonna took over the world and with each release and tour both our friendship and working relationhip grew stronger. I value her opinion on PR more than any other.

When Liz stopped working with Madonna in 2014, we would all often proclaim: what would Liz do? In February 2015 Madonna tumbled down the stairs at the O2 in London while singing 'Living for Love' at the BRIT Awards show. I was watching the from the side of the arena with her new US PR, the equally wonderful, Brian Bumbery, who turned to me as we ran backstage and said: 'WE GOTTA CALL

LIZ!!' I'll never forget the thud her head made when it hit the stage. It was a really scary moment.

Luckily Madonna was OK and the next day taped an entire Jonathan Ross TV special. When she forgot a lyric in rehearsal she laughed it off saying, 'Actually I fell on my head last night.' And when they recorded the show and she made her entrance onto the set, she stopped at the steps, poking fun at the night before. Incredibly, she then threw a party at Annabel's, a very upmarket private members' club in Berkeley Square, for her dancers and team. Twenty-four hours after falling onstage, she was dancing at the club as champagne and cosmopolitans flowed.

You have to have a sense of humour to do this for a living. And you have to keep everything in perspective even when operating in the rarefied air of someone as big as Madonna. Whenever I was in New York City, I would visit Liz in her amazing twentieth-floor corner office at the Time-Warner Rockefeller Plaza building. On one wall of her office, a bit like mine back in London, were framed Madonna newspaper and magazine covers. Unlike my office, however, Liz had a bank of hairdryers, just like the old-school ones in beauty salons, that had featured on Madonna's Blonde Ambition Tour, and three bright blue chairs used as props during that tour's 'Material Girl' production. The office also had a panoramic view of New York City to die for.

Years later while we were in NYC doing promo with Madonna for her *Hard Candy* album, Liz and I had tickets to see Patti LuPone in *Gypsy*, which we were very much looking forward to. Like me, Liz is a massive musical theatre fan. Madonna was doing some TV at Dylan's Candy Bar, near Bloomingdale's, and she was running late. As the clock ticked closer and closer to the 7.30 curtain we were slightly in a panic. Miraculously, we got to the theatre just before the curtain went up. However, the ushers would not let us take our seats, and asked us to stand at the back of the stalls. Liz and I are both what I would call 'don't fuck with us' kind of women and were protesting when suddenly Patti LuPone herself walked right past us, singing her way down the aisle to the stage to start the show. Suddenly it all became clear. Thank God we didn't make a scene!

Liz and I worked on other acts together, most notably k.d. Lang, so we talked often and laughed frequently. In those days Madonna was barely out of the news so we ran up big phone bills while putting out PR fires. k.d. Lang was another discovery by Seymour Stein of Sire Records. She first came over to the UK in the late eighties with a cowpunk album (*Angel with a Lariat*) from her native Canada, lacking confidence but with an incredible voice. We went to the Rasa Sayang in Soho for lunch to get to know each other. It was one of the first Thai restaurants in London, certainly the first time I ever had Thai food, and we'd often take artists there for bonding lunches and dinners. Another record company haunt was a classic Greek restaurant off Charlotte Street where they not only let you break the plates but literally encouraged you to do so. The place was hugely popular with rock bands.

A few albums later k.d. unveiled her masterpiece, *Ingenue*, with the global smash hit 'Constant Craving' and the rest was history. Liz did that infamous *Vanity Fair* cover where Cindy Crawford is giving k.d. Lang a shave in a barber's chair, her face covered in shaving cream.

By 1992 Madonna published her first book, not surprisingly called *Sex*, an explicit coffee-table book of photographs. It came wrapped in a silver-foil sleeve and the reviewers had to go to the publisher and sign a confidentiality agreement before they could read it. Basically, the book was under lock and key, the secrecy around it immense. The book created a national furore and made the 10 o'clock news. It went on sale at midnight and the queues at the bookshops brave enough to stock it went around the block. I still have an unopened copy of *Sex* which I might need to sell if this book doesn't do well. The accompanying album *Erotica* carried on both the theme and the innuendo.

Madonna toured *Erotica* the following year with The Girlie Show, which opened in September 1993 at Wembley Stadium, by now Madonna's second home. For the show she wore a radio mike to one side and I remember putting the photographers from all the papers I didn't like on that side of the huge pit (these were the days when Madonna let photographers shoot her from the pit, not miles back) and the photographers from papers I liked, who I knew would showcase the photos really well on their front page, like the *Guardian*, on the side with no mike. It made me laugh to exact some long overdue revenge on some of the papers who had been less than cooperative and/or supportive of Madonna.

By now, Madonna mania was in full swing. She used to stay at what was the Hyde Park Hotel, now the Mandarin Oriental, across the street from Harvey Nichols in Knightsbridge. Police barricades were up for blocks and crowds were so big you couldn't find the store entrance, let alone see it. She liked the hotel primarily because she could go out the back and drive off without the hordes of photographers out the front following her. Or go for a run in Hyde Park, where journalists so desperate for a story would try to keep pace with her and her equally fit bodyguards. Madonna mania was so insane that hundreds of photographers would greet her arrival at Heathrow. Once her car ran over *Sun* photographer Dave Hogan's foot (accidentally) when leaving

Heathrow and he dined out on that story for years!

That September the Pet Shop Boys had a big party at the Roundhouse just before Madonna's show, and I felt rather hung-over the following day when I had to go to Wembley to ensure all was OK with various press issues. It was great to see lots of old friends from the *Smash Hits* era at the party.

By this time my dad was nearing the end but he miraculously hung on till after Madonna had opened in London. After the shows, I flew home and my sister arrived from New York. They say people intuitively hang on till their loved ones are present and I must say that was the case with my dad. My sister had gone for a walk, my mom was downstairs paying some bills and I was upstairs in my parents' bedroom with my dad, the Chicago Cubs baseball game playing quietly in the background. He was pretty weak by then; we had hospice care because he wanted to die at home. 'The Cubs will win the World Series where you're going,' I told him. And with that he peacefully passed with a smile on his face. It was quite surreal and incredibly moving.

Years later, in 2016, the Cubs actually *did* win the World Series. For years they were the joke of baseball, having gone a hundred years without winning it, the longest time between wins ever. I was lucky enough to go to the first two World Series home games in Chicago at Wrigley Field and thought of my dad throughout both games, often teary eyed (not because they lost them both). I met lots of similar people that magical weekend who had lost loved ones and never thought they would see the Cubs in a World Series. It remains one of the best things I've ever been to and my dad was with me every step of the way.

A year later my mom gave me and my sister a bit of money, after my dad's will was settled. I thought of all the sensible things I could do with the money. Instead, I flew

Concorde to Barbados for a week. Every night, I'd watch the sunset from my balcony, listening to Oasis and drinking rum punch. My dad wouldn't have wanted it any other way.

The second thing I did with the money was join the Groucho Club. It was the first private members' club in London and everyone who was anyone wanted to join. And it wasn't easy. You had to be approved by the membership committee and they were very particular about getting the balance right. Not too many music business reprobates, theatre snobs, newspaper editors, etc. Luckily for me, both Janet Street-Porter and Neil Tennant were members and they recommended me. I was in! However, there was still a one-year waiting list unless you wanted to join for life for £2,000. Assuming I would live more than five more years, it seemed an absolute bargain.

It proved to be a valuable investment as I am still a member and haven't had to pay anything since. Back in the eighties and most of the nineties, the Groucho was the place to be. One minute you were drinking in an upstairs bar and indulging in the odd line of cocaine and the next they were kicking you out at 3 a.m. Walking down the stairs you wondered why on earth the club was dark and no one else was there. Those were the days when Keith Allen and Damien Hirst held court among many other well-known musicians, actors, authors and even politicians. It was a heady mix of people who regularly frequented the place. Late one night, Madness frontman Suggs took us through a secret upstairs passageway, up and down stairs and outside staircases that somehow, mysteriously, led to a small drinking club, the Colony Room, next door that his mother used to go to.

There was something poetic about using the money my dad had left me to join the Groucho Club as he absolutely adored the Marx Brothers. Of course, Groucho was his favourite.

Malibu, c.1993
Left to right: Liz Rosenberg, k.d. Lang, BC

Chapter 8

Constant Craving

By the late eighties Warner Brothers had signed both REM and Elvis Costello and I was beyond excited. The only problem was that by now the company had split in two, with separate US and UK set-ups, and I was working the UK side. Much to my frustration, I had to watch from afar, or at least another floor, as Elvis and REM, two of my favourite artists, were close but not close enough.

Elvis's label debut in 1989 was *Spike*, an album led by the hit single 'Veronica', which he co-wrote with Paul McCartney, while REM opened their Warner Brothers account with the mighty *Green*, their first, 'almost but not quite', big hit album, in late '88. To say I was green with envy that I couldn't work both these projects would be a massive understatement.

REM played their first UK shows in 1984 at the Marquee and I went to both nights, thanks to some friends who worked at IRS, their original indie label. They remain two of the best shows I've ever seen. Michael Stipe was the most engaging, enigmatic frontman I'd seen in years, while the band, especially guitarist Peter Buck, were just a thing of beauty to behold. They were an American rock band with British ideals, a marriage of transatlantic influences, and I absolutely adored them.

I'd seen Elvis Costello with the Attractions in their early days, most memorably at Brunel University, where they tore through a massive setlist in lightning-quick speed. And I was at the Royal Albert Hall, with an orchestra, for his majestic, country-tinged *Almost Blue* opus. I was in a box with Linda Stein, wife (at the time) of Sire founder Seymour Stein, and almost as loud, funny and New York City brash as her husband. The trouble was, Linda could not stop talking during the show, fuelled by the well-stocked bar in our box, and during some of the quieter songs, like the gorgeous, bittersweet 'Good Year for the Roses', her voice was almost as loud as Elvis's. And he had a microphone! Mind you, I'm one to talk! I've spent many a show being told to be quiet, mostly by friends. There's something about Americans – we were just born to make ourselves heard.

As WEA was now two companies, there were, of course, two different press offices. We were all housed in the Electric Lighting Station, off Kensington High Street on Kensington Court, almost opposite the Royal Garden Hotel and in spitting distance of Kensington Gardens. Before we moved to Kensington, a promising sixteen-year-old came to work in the press office on a government-backed YTS training scheme. She was soon offered a full-time job as a press-office junior and at that tender age had to make a choice between working for me or working for the other head of press, Lee Ellen Newman – separate but still one nation under a groove. We both interviewed Denise. My competition told her, and I quote, 'BC will eat you alive.'

Such kind words! But as luck would have it, Denise read something that very same day that said: if it excites you and scares you at the same time, it probably means you should do it. Wisely she took that advice and with it the job and stayed working for me for the next ten years. She was from

Woolwich, and her working-class family was completely different from my upbringing and my life. She was totally unfazed by celebrity, and not at all put off by managers or record company executives who erred on the side of being a bully. She had the best kind of smarts: common sense. And because of it, was a natural. She kept me grounded, and to this day still does. I remember her coming back from getting me a few things at Marks & Spencer one day, and heard her telling the team: 'You'll never believe what they have, washed lettuce for £1.50 a bag! Who would buy that?' Guilty as charged.

Eventually my PA moved on and I decided to give Denise a chance and promote her. She wasn't quite ready for the step up, but my gut feeling said we should give it a go. The first month was a bumpy ride but I knew it was going to work when I came in one day and she had a big Post-it stuck on her computer with a list that said: '10 things to make Denise's life easier.' She understood what it took to do the job and was determined to make it work.

She says those early days were like the opening scene in *The Devil Wears Prada* where Anne Hathaway is desperately trying to get the right coffee for Meryl Streep and have it on her desk before she arrives at the office. Both big fans of *Absolutely Fabulous*, we would joke about me being Eddy, the Jennifer Saunders character in their cracking PR firm, and her being Bubble, the rather ditzy assistant. But she wasn't at all ditzy.

Jennifer Saunders is one of my absolute role models. I loved *French and Saunders* and saw them in the early days at the Raymond Revuebar in Soho. I happily devoured each and every episode of their groundbreaking TV series and was equally smitten with *Absolutely Fabulous*. It was incredibly funny, and not just because her character ran a PR firm. I still laugh rewatching the very first episode where they were desperately struggling to get celebrities to attend an event. 'Darling, I need names, names, names,' she demanded. Exactly.

She's a wonderful writer and an incredibly insightful chronicler of the times. There's a classic moment in *Absolutely Fabulous* when her character Eddy doesn't win the PR Person of the Year Award and she inches her chair and entire table closer and closer to the stage until they say someone else's name. The way she parodies PR, fame, celebrity, family and everything in between is so on the money.

When the Pet Shop Boys recorded the single 'Absolutely Fabulous' in 1994, I was lucky enough to meet Jennifer Saunders and she was everything I could have hoped for. Smart, clever women are to be cherished and applauded.

To this day, Denise is one of my best friends. I've been to her wedding, albeit very hung-over after a long, boozy dinner with Michael Stipe the night before. And proudly been the first person to take each of her three daughters to the theatre or a concert for their first time (*The Lion King*, *Mary Poppins*, Olly Murs). And on that very hot day of her summer wedding, a long Catholic ceremony in a sweltering church, I had a car pick me up after the reception to go to the massive REM headline show at Milton Keynes, the first of two nights, at an enormous outdoor space just outside London. By that time, the company structure had flip-flopped once again, and thankfully I was now working on the US side, reunited with Madonna and reacquainted with both Elvis Costello and REM.

The company had now outgrown the Electric Lighting Station and the entire operation moved to a purpose-built building round the corner on Kensington Church Street. I had a big office and a relatively big team. The best part of our floor was a large room with sofas and leather chairs called the Think Tank. You were supposed to go there when feeling creative (to think!) but we used it primarily for artist interviews and it was especially useful for sneaky lunchtime naps when suffering from the night before.

Those were good times. Computers replaced fax machines, mobile phones that were the size of a cassette replaced those original shoe-sized phones and the CD had long replaced vinyl. Record sales were booming and the industry was thriving. I always wanted to keep the artists in-house but sometimes they hired independent PRs. Of course now it's the opposite as I am independent, but back then you stubbornly fought to keep the talent. One new American act, Deee-Lite, had an incredible song called 'Groove Is in the Heart'. It was obvious it was going to be a massive hit and I was crushed when they hired an independent. The manager said he had sent me an email but had never heard back. A what? So much for the future.

The first Elvis Costello album I did the press for was *Mighty Like a Rose* in 1991 and we have worked together on almost every album he's made since, and he's made a lot of albums. Elvis had a rather massive beard then, as portrayed on the cover of that album, and he often joked that the disappointing reviews were down to the beard. He followed it with his first foray into the classical world, with the enthralling *Juliet Letters* with the Brodsky Quartet, based on Shakespearean sonnets, and review wise, normal service was resumed.

Elvis is a massive Liverpool fan and these days we spend much of our time talking about the Premier League. Even though he's the guy who wrote 'I Don't Want to Go to Chelsea', I've forgiven him.

The first REM album I worked on was released that same year and was their big breakthrough, led by the single 'Losing My Religion'. The band came over to the UK to promote the forthcoming *Out of Time* album and were scheduled to do two intimate shows at the Borderline, a small club, now sadly closed, off Charring Cross Road, under the moniker Bingo Hand Job. They hadn't yet seen the landmark video for 'Losing My Religion', so when it arrived from the US by courier (something of a novelty back then), we all gathered in Moira's office, by now the managing director, to watch it. This was such a pivotal moment in the band's career, and the video, like the song, became part of the furniture in 1991. Michael Stipe had stepped out of the band and into the stratosphere with that video, and in a musical landscape dictated by MTV, they, like Madonna, led the charge. Watching Michael watch himself in that video, taking notes to be relayed to the director on changes he wanted made to the video, was an education in itself.

The shows were as hot (literally) as the Stones' Toronto club shows. I took some press out before the show for food and drinks and splurged on very expensive white Burgundy. However, once inside the club, I made the cardinal sin of drinking the house wine (to call it wine is really taking a liberty) and suffered enormously the next day. From that point on, I made it a rule to only drink vodka and tonic in clubs. But like a trouper, I was there for the second night, which was recorded. The queues were round the block for the fan-club-only event, and the excitement was palpable. The setlist was insane, spanning their career thus far, and numbered almost thirty songs in well over two hours of blistering rock 'n' roll. Not just Georgia's finest, America's absolute best. And the UK took REM to heart, propelling that album to the top of the charts.

Michael Stipe had decided not to do any press interviews for *Out of Time* and continued his media silence with the 1992 release of the even more successful *Automatic for the*

People. This was an unprecedented stance for the main man of a band just on the cusp of the big time to adopt. Everyone wanted to interview Michael but he was not available. Instead they spoke with Mike Mills and Peter Buck. This unorthodox approach to interviews could easily have backfired but the music was incredibly strong; sales kept on rising, the songs were all over the radio and the videos in constant rotation on MTV. By the time Michael started to do interviews again, the band had become one of the biggest bands in the world. By not doing interviews, fans and critics were even more interested in him. It added to his mystique.

The band also did not tour either of those albums, another highly unusual move in that current climate, but they always moved to the beat of a different drum. Not touring for six years paid massive dividends for them personally and professionally when they finally did resurface in 1995, taking those two albums on the road. They couldn't sell out the shows fast enough, hence those two nights at Milton Keynes Bowl in summer 1995.

As Michael was not doing interviews, Peter Buck and Mike Mills came to the UK often to talk to the press. Over the course of two years I got to know them both extremely well. We shared many enjoyable dinners, perhaps the most noteworthy being at Leith's in Notting Hill, when the WEA Chairman Rob Dickins made the mistake of letting Mike Mills order any wine he wanted to celebrate the incredible success of *Automatic for the People* (over two million sold in the UK). Mike didn't hesitate, and immediately asked for a bottle of Château d'Yquem, the most expensive dessert wine on the planet. We must have had two bottles as there were about fifteen of us. It was delicious. Mike even insisted that the waiter try it.

Artist dinners were a normal occurrence, and the bigger

the artist, the better the restaurant. These were exclusive affairs with barely more than ten people – heads of department, artist, manager. Not surprisingly they usually put me next to the artist, especially if the artist was a little bit on the difficult side. Not only could I usually engage them in conversation but most likely had spent much of the day overseeing their interviews. I was also charged with ordering the wine, at which by now I had become something of an expert in by the best possible way: trial and error!

We had dinners with Donald Fagen (Steely Dan), Randy Newman, Joni Mitchell, k.d. Lang and many others but one of the most memorable was with Neil Young. It was unusual for him to do interviews and even more so to dine with the record label so we were all super excited and a little bit apprehensive. Neil was accompanied by his long-time manager, the late, great Elliott Roberts, who was very smart but not smart enough to know when to stop wearing leather trousers!

Neil was a bit grumpy when they arrived at Leith's and the chairman asked Neil how that day's interviews had gone. He mumbled something about writers reading too much into the lyrics and I said, did they ask about 'The Emperor of Wyoming', the first track on his debut album and an instrumental? This immediately broke the ice as it showed we were real fans. It really made him laugh, helped no doubt by the very expensive Chardonnay I had ordered.

Because Michael Stipe was MIA from promo for two albums, I didn't really get to know him until the band toured *Monster* in 1995. Certain artists have a charisma that's otherworldly, usually the lead singer, and Stipe had it in spades. A press darling, one journalist put it succinctly when he said: 'Michael is so charming and funny until the tape recorder is turned on.' Michael speaks slowly sometimes and leaves gaps in conversation when he is thinking about what to say next.

Journalists have a tendency to rush into those spaces, probably out of nerves, with more questions, instead of letting him finish his thought. He is very bright and very funny. Once while on tour, after another incredible show where I had generously helped myself to the wine in Peter Buck's dressing room, Stipe pointed at my lips and said with a straight face: 'Red-wine lip, not a good look!'

I remember first hearing the seminal Radiohead album *The Bends* when Michael played me the haunting 'High and Dry' in the tour bus parked backstage in Chicago. Back in London we once had dinner with Thom Yorke at The Ivy. Cherished times. Being from Chicago, it was amazing to return to my home town with the UK press in tow to see and interview REM. At one Chicago show, Michael dedicated a song to me and I was really touched.

I travelled around Europe and the US with the band and assorted journalists for the next five years. It was a wonderful time and I never failed to enjoy the show. They remain one of the great live bands and for a time, in 1995 and 1996, they were the biggest band in the world. Their headline Glastonbury performances are historic.

By now, football and music were colliding in new and exciting ways. Comedians David Baddiel (Chelsea) and Frank Skinner (West Bromwich Albion) invented a riveting new TV format called *Fantasy Football* which had a great three-year run on Channel 4. It featured David and Frank, flatmates at the time, sitting round the studio as if it were their flat, with other like-minded celebrity guests talking about the beautiful game. I'm not quite sure how, but I got myself on an early guest list and soon became a permanent fixture in the show's green room where I met so many comedians, musicians and footballers and became quite friendly with David and Frank.

In 1996 England hosted the Euros. I'd never been one to care much for the health of the national team, as club football was where my heart lay, but it was impossible not to get caught up with the excitement of the tournament being held on home soil. David and Frank, along with the Lightning Seeds' Ian Broudie, wrote and recorded the now classic 'Football's Coming Home' which became an anthem for the tournament and is still played every time England are in a World Cup or the Euros.

Rod Stewart was on Warner Brothers and had recorded the Scottish team song, which we released. It fell to me, being such a football fan, to liaise with Paul Stretford, who looked after the Scottish national team, and we became good friends. He got me a ticket for the England v. Scotland game at Wembley, for which I will be forever grateful.

Rod is a massive Celtic fan and really loves the game. Once while we were in Sweden to shoot a *Rolling Stone* cover, he asked me to read him the scores of that Saturday's UK top-flight games backstage before a show. I ran through the scores, leaving off Chelsea's 7–0 thrashing by Nottingham Forest. The next day before I left Stockholm, my phone rang, and the voice just said 'seven–nil!!!!' and laughed. Rod hung up before I could get a word in.

England beat Scotland in the Euros, and enjoyed an unusually good run, driven by Paul Gascoigne, Alan Shearer and Teddy Sheringham. They made the quarter-finals where they beat the Netherlands and then lost in the semi-finals on penalties to Germany. I went to both games at Wembley and the semi-final loss was just heartbreaking. From euphoria to total despair within minutes, there is little sadder than a stadium full of fans walking out of a ground in total silence.

My mother was visiting and staying at my flat. After the match, we had all gone back to Gascoigne's, a small wine bar owned by Depeche Mode's Andy Fletcher in St John's Wood, just off Abbey Road, to console ourselves after the loss. Andy and his wife were part of my Chelsea gang, and we always went to the games together. It was quite late by the time I walked home and my mother was furious, worried that something bad had happened to me. Yes mom, something bad did happen! *We lost!*

Chelsea FC training ground – Blue Day video shoot,
May 1977
Left to right: Dennis Wise (captain), BC, Suggs,
Mark Hughes

Chapter 9
True Blue

As the BBC newsreaders used to say when they got to the football, if you don't want to know the results, look away now! Fast-forward to the bit in this chapter about Madonna if that's the case. Though if you like Suggs, the inimitable Madness frontman, you're fine. And if you like football, you don't need to leave the room to make a cup of tea, so read on!

Much to my surprise and delight, Chelsea blew the cobwebs off that England Euro loss when they won the FA Cup the following year in 1997, for the first time since 1970. I'd been to a Chelsea FA Cup final in 1994, when what started as a wonderful sunny day ended in massive disappointment amid torrential rain as we lost 4–0 to Manchester United. Yet another dark day at Wembley Stadium.

Chelsea had also played something called the Full Members' Cup final against Manchester City (who were crap then) in 1986. I couldn't wait for the game as it would be my first trip to Wembley Stadium. The day before the match was my birthday and, as it fell dangerously on a Saturday, was an almost twenty-four-hour marathon of fun. I'd had a nice long, boozy lunch with friends followed by dinner at Orso in Covent Garden with Moira and Paul Conroy. We were going to promoter Harvey Goldsmith's fortieth birthday party, which was to be a star-studded affair as he was the

UK's leading music promoter at the time, best known as the man who helped Bob Geldof make Live Aid a reality. We'd only got round to ordering when suddenly there was a bit of a kerfuffle followed by the arrival of Madonna and Sean Penn who, after saying a sheepish hi, sat a couple of tables away from us.

As if this wasn't enough excitement for one evening, when we got to the party, Pete Townshend was there, and for some reason I felt duty bound to show him how I could play air guitar. Such a good look! Suffice to say I felt absolutely dreadful the following morning but gamely went to the restaurant in Wembley where we were all meeting for a pre-game lunch. One look at the smoked salmon starter did it for me and I made my excuses and left, beating a hasty retreat to the sanctuary of my bed. It must have been some game, as we won 5–4!

By 1997 we were finally in the FA Cup final. At last! Back then the FA Cup was without doubt the most exciting competition for virtually all UK football fans. The entire country practically ground to a halt on Cup-final day. The Champions League hadn't really exploded yet – most fans didn't even dream of that. But give us a good FA Cup run and we were beyond happy. We'd sit by the TV waiting for the draw for the next round, praying we'd be home not away and, if the latter, happy to travel to Sheffield or Wolverhampton. It was all about the day out, the lunch before, the giddy excitement after, post-match drinks. The camaraderie among the supporters was fantastic. Games on TV were more of a rarity then; you pretty much lived for *Match of the Day* on Saturday night and usually the only way to see the game was to go to the game. Otherwise you sat glued to the radio.

People talk about the magic of the FA Cup and it really is true, though heavily diluted now as there are so many different cup competitions and there is so much football on TV. Back then there was little more exciting. People who didn't even like football would have friends and family round on cup-final day. It was a bit like Wimbledon – a must-see national event. Coverage on TV started at 9 a.m., complete with interviewers outside the team hotels, the coach journey to Wembley, all live on both BBC and ITV. It was intoxicating. I never dreamt that I would see Chelsea win the FA Cup let alone the Champions League and the Premier League, but let's save those successes for later.

As fate would have it, about a month before the cup final, the relatively unknown songwriter Mike Connaris brought me a track he thought was perfect for Suggs. I'd known Suggs through Paul Conroy during all the initial Madness success. Suggs is a massive Chelsea fan, so our paths often crossed at games. We shared one memorable night and very early morning at one of the first ever Q Awards. By 1990, buoyed by its success, Q took the rather unusual step for a magazine of holding a yearly awards ceremony. It quickly became commonplace. The first Q Awards was at Greek Street jazz club Ronnie Scott's, the second at Abbey Road Studios and the third at the St James's Hotel, the last of their relatively small awards celebrations before it moved to the Park Lane Hotel and later the Grosvenor House, with the bulk of the labels, lots of journalists and wall-to-wall rock stars always in attendance.

What made the awards ceremony even more unusual was that it started at lunchtime and was over by 3 p.m., when the serious drinking really started and various after-shows took place. By 9 p.m. it felt like 4 a.m. Total carnage. What made it so special was that it really felt like it was exclusively for the artists, the journalists and PR people like me. It was our day, and one we cherished and looked forward to every year, though we grew to dread the morning after. Artist turnout was exclusively A-list and the award really meant something, especially to the artists who were critically acclaimed but not commercially successful.

The second year I brought Lou Reed, who had flown over from NYC on Concorde the night before to accept an award. We were also working with Seal at the time, who had just exploded with 'Kiss from a Rose', and the party back at Trevor Horn's Notting Hill ZTT office was off the hook. I couldn't even get out of bed the next morning, so when ZTT sent over a bottle of champagne as a thank you with a Jackson Pollock card that read: 'This is how my head feels' it made me laugh! It was exactly how my head felt.

Obviously Lou didn't go to the party. Lou was not an after-party type of guy. I once took *NME* to New York City to do a cover story on Lou. The writer and I spent four days waiting for Lou to agree to do the interview – typical Lou fun and games driven by his love/hate relationship with the press (they loved him, he hated them). He finally agreed to do the interview at Nobu in Greenwich Village, which was all the rage at the time as it had only just opened. He ordered an exorbitantly priced bottle of wine, knowing the label would pick up the tab, almost $1000. When the writer later mentioned the wine in the story, Lou went mental. The manager called me to complain about this, which was just a bunch of hot air. Why wouldn't the writer write about it? Why would Lou behave like that if he didn't want the writer to write about it? It was all for show.

Much to our surprise, Lou asked us if we wanted to go to a party with him as we left Nobu, so we got into his waiting town car. He immediately took us to a Gray's Papaya hot dog stand, an NYC institution, and insisted the writer try their infamous hot dogs even though we had just eaten a very pricey Japanese dinner. The massive contrast between the pricey Nobu and cheap Gray's Papaya was not lost on anyone. Another show. No sooner had we chowed down on the dogs than Lou decided he was done and got dropped off at home. It was almost as if he was afraid of revealing too much. His friend, however, took us to the party anyway. David Geffen was there. It was surreal.

On another promo trip to London, Lou insisted that he sit at a desk, facing north, for all the interviews and that the writer face him, both of them sitting on very stiff, formal chairs, creating an aura that was way more intimidating than necessary. He thrived on that. Writers were in fear of him when they arrived for their encounter. But that *NME* trip was memorable.

After the St James's Hotel *Q* Awards ceremony there was a very small after-show in the penthouse of the hotel. I was looking after Rod Stewart on the day and Suggs was also there. Rod and Suggs got on like a proverbial house on fire as they both love football, so there was much good-humoured banter. For me, there was also a fair bit of cocaine, something of a necessity when you start drinking at twelve! The suite had an outside rooftop where we all ended up, drinking and talking absolute rubbish. Rod was kind enough to agree to say hello to more than a few writers' parents who they eagerly called to say: I'm standing here with Rod Stewart and you can speak to him! Rod was a really good sport and happily said hi. It was insane fun and quite a night.

When all the Madness stopped, Suggs signed a solo deal with Warner Brothers and in 1995 released his first solo album, *The Lone Ranger*. It was really nice to finally have the opportunity to work together. Mike Connaris reckoned that his song, the aptly named 'Blue Day', would be the perfect vehicle for Suggs and would make a great FA Cup-final song. Back then each team that got to the final did their own FA Cup song and some of them even made the top 30. Suggs loved the track, as did the club. I somehow managed to convince WEA to pay for the recording and to put it out as a single. Everything happened so quickly. Before you could say dreams really do come true, I was in a London studio on a Sunday afternoon with Chelsea captain Dennis Wise, Gianluca Vialli, Mark Hughes, Steve Clarke, Gianfranco Zola and the entire Chelsea team making a record. When the team left, Suggs and I sat around having a beer, practically speechless, literally in dreamland, not believing what had just happened. It was a real pinch-me moment.

The accompanying video was shot mostly in the studio and at the club's training ground near Heathrow. Just going to training was a thrill in itself; Suggs and Mark Hughes (ex-Man United, then a Chelsea player) had a kick-about, plus Suggs and Chelsea captain Dennis Wise mugged it up for the camera. Dennis was the most receptive to the record and everything that went with it and couldn't have been nicer or more welcoming to us. He was the kind of player opposition fans moaned about but were desperate to have on their team. Looking back at the video now, twenty-five years later, there's a lot of joy, youth and innocence in that studio.

My brief career in A & R was a rousing success as the single charted at 22. Buoyed by this result, my football follow-up, a track with Manchester United superstar striker Andy Cole, who Paul Stretford managed, sank without trace and I beat a hasty retreat back to my comfort zone world of PR. There I stayed, until a brief spell in management, so stay tuned.

As if it was written in the stars, Chelsea won the FA Cup, beating Middlesbrough 2–0 and scoring what was then the fastest ever goal, in the first minute of the game. That in itself was incredibly exciting as was hearing 'Blue Day' blasted on the Wembley tannoy, which brought tears to my eyes. The song is now part of Chelsea folklore and is played at every home game and any big final. It's our theme song. A banner still hangs over the Matthew Harding Stand at Stamford Bridge declaring: 'The only place to be every other Saturday' – the song's opening line – 'is walking down the Fulham Road'. For some reason I always cry or at least well up when Chelsea win a big game or even score a great goal. Like music, football is incredibly emotional, which is such a big part of its appeal.

Suggs traditionally rented a flatbed truck or an open-top bus for Cup-final days, something he could transport all his rowdy mates to Wembley on as they drank their way to the ground. My lot had a bunch of tables at the Hilton next door and indulged in drink and drugs. Here's some handy advice: don't ever take cocaine before or during a football game. All it does is make you even more stressed and anxious about the result. The two just don't mix! These were the days before corporate hospitality took over football. There was an innocence, a tradition to uphold, and much fun to be had that will never be repeated since the advent of what Roy Keane so famously dubbed the prawn-sandwich brigade.

After the game, wild celebrations understandably erupted, and being involved in the record made the occasion even more memorable. The icing on the cake however was when Dennis Wise invited me and Suggs to the players' celebrations at the Waldorf Hotel, on the Aldwych in London. By the time Suggs and I arrived we were very much worse for wear, not sure we could string a sentence together but so happy to be there, two star-struck football fans who couldn't believe their luck. How I got home is a total mystery and why I decided to cycle to the victory parade in Chelsea the following day, on very little sleep, made no sense either. Not surprisingly I took a tumble going round Hyde Park. Happy but bruised.

Shortly after Chelsea won the FA Cup, Suggs and I were invited to lunch with the Chelsea chairman Ken Bates and his lovely partner Suzannah. Ken and I became quite friendly and frequently had lunch, usually at Langan's Brasserie in Mayfair. He was quite a character. The most un-PC person I had every met but with a Chelsea heart of gold. He sold the club to Roman Abramovich in 2003 and the rest is history. So thank you, Ken!

When Chelsea started their own in-house radio and TV station, Suggs and I were asked to guest on the first matchday show. Suggs hadn't been to bed and arrived straight from a big boozy night out. Our interview quickly disintegrated into a very amusing car crash. We were not on air for long. Nor were we asked back.

Later that summer, Diana, Princess of Wales died, and the whole of the Kensington area where Warners was based became a sea of mourning, with thousands of floral tributes and wreaths and people flocking to pay their respects day after day. The office was round the corner from Kensington Palace and the entire park and surrounding streets were transformed into a massive tribute to Diana, which multiplied daily as it grew larger and larger. The owner of the flower stall on the corner of Kensington Church Street and Kensington High Street must have bought a Caribbean island with the profits.

Life for the Queen of Pop – her Madgesty as the UK press dubbed Madonna – had hit something of a bumpy patch, her first. Her 1994 album *Bedtime Stories* wasn't as well received critically or commercially as previous singles and albums. Always one to thrive on reinvention, Madonna came back fighting with a starring role in the film *Evita* and a smash hit in 1997 with 'Don't Cry for Me Argentina'. Talk about reinvention! No one, however, could have predicted what came next – the 1998 masterpiece that is *Ray of Light*. Her collaboration with producer William Orbit hit new heights even for Madonna. I had worked with William on his own adventurous recordings – an album appropriately called *Pieces in a Modern Style* – so it was very helpful that I knew him when the album exploded.

Before *Ray of Light* was released, WEA were having meetings in London with all the heads of the various European record companies. Madonna arranged a playback for them to preview the album in a studio. Liz Rosenberg was there, as was Moira, now managing director of Warner UK, and they both insisted I come too. Along with Madonna, and her manager Caresse Henry, we were the only women in the room. There was a real air of excitement and nervous energy as Madonna played the album to a room full of record company executives. She sat onstage at the front, and everyone was given some paper to write down their thoughts on the new music. When it finished, Madonna asked what the first single should be. Silence. Uncomfortable silence. No one wanted to go first or give an opinion. None of these high-powered men spoke. Finally, just to break the silence, I raised my hand, suggesting the incredible song 'Drowned World / Substitute for Love', which seemed to bridge the Madonna of old and the Madonna of now. In the end the first single was the ballad 'Frozen', but at least I spoke up. Chalk one up for girl power.

Another artist Liz Rosenberg and I worked on together was Cher, who had her first Warner Brothers album around the same time as *Ray of Light* and scored a massive global smash with 'Believe'. Sadly, Liz didn't come to the UK with Cher in January for the Harrods sale. The Knightsbridge department store used to have celebrities open their summer and winter sales. Sometimes the artists would arrive riding a horse or in a horse-drawn carriage – it was always a little bit mad. Those were real paparazzi moments. And so, on the back of the incredible success of 'Believe', Cher opened the Harrods sale in January 1999. She was invited to shop in the store after it had closed the night before the sale and consequently Moira and I found ourselves walking round the whole of an empty Harrods with Cher, grabbing some pre-sale bargains. Definitely one of the more surreal experiences we have had but tremendous fun. The funny part was we couldn't take our purchases home that night, and had to collect them the following day once the sale had officially begun. Cher is really funny and did a very amusing commentary of the clothes on sale, the must-have items and the must-not-have items on our journey round the store.

By the time we'd all partied like it was 1999 (thank you, Prince), and the new millennium had begun, I was starting to think more and more about leaving the label and starting out on my own. So much in the industry and at the label had changed since I'd arrived, fresh faced and eager back in early eighties. Back then there were no computers and of course now we were teched up. In the summer of 2000, a new kind of reality show arrived on our shores called *Big Brother*. It was so popular that when one of the characters, Nasty Nick, was kicked out of the house for a shocking bout of duplicity which was pure TV gold, the whole press office gathered round one computer screen to watch the proceedings. It was the first time any of us had actually watched something live on a computer and showed just how much life had changed. And that was just the beginning.

Around that same time, the new chairman decided to bring in a new MD for the Warner Brothers label and Moira was gone. For me, the writing was on the wall and we decided to start our own independent PR company. I resigned shortly after but had to work out a couple of months' notice. Madonna was about to release yet another ground-breaking album, *Music*, and as she'd just given birth in LA to Rocco, the launch party was there.

While Moira looked for office space, I flew to LA for the launch with the *Sun*'s Bizarre editor Dominic Mohan. I had brought a tiny Chelsea shirt with ROCCO on the back as a present, and as Dom and I were ushered over to see Madonna at the party, he asked if he could give it to Madonna as a gift from the *Sun*. Not one to shy away from good PR I agreed. And two days later Madonna was on the front page of the *Sun* holding a Chelsea shirt! Blue is the colour!

As I was leaving WEA on such good terms, I was allowed to keep my company car (an Audi) and worked out a deal to take some of my artists with me (Madonna, REM, Rod Stewart) to my new company, MBC, a wonderful abbreviation of both Moira's and my name. It also sounded important, like the BBC, or NBC, and the snappy logo was flag-like in its red, white and blue design. My time in the big Warner Brothers house was finally up. It had been quite a ride, and almost two decades of fun. I left on the last Friday in October and drove a few boxes of BC memorabilia over to our new space in a self-serviced office in St John's Wood, ready and excited about what lay ahead.

Independence Day: BC and Moira Bellas at *Concert for George*, Royal Albert Hall, 29 November 2002

Chapter 10
Independence Day

It was all a bit of a shock to the system. If the phones didn't work, there was no one to come fix them. If the internet was down, there was no IT department to come sort it out. We were on our own. Me, Moira and Paul Conroy's eighteen-year-old son Drew, who had never worked in an office, doing work experience. The three of us, all in one room, just off reception in our new space, a self-serviced office in St John's Wood, just down the road from Lord's Cricket Ground. It was small, but it was ours. And we loved it.

One thing we didn't have to worry about was the media knowing how to get in touch with us because from the very first minute we stepped into the new office, the phone did not stop ringing. Non-stop, literally off the hook, calls all day. And the reason? That day's *Daily Star* carried a front-page headline that declared: 'Madonna to Marry at Skibo' – which was a luxury castle hotel in Scotland.

Was it true? Yes! Was it a secret? Yes! She was marrying Guy Ritchie, and in the run-up to the wedding had become something of an honorary Brit. We spent most of our first day at MBC fielding calls. In fact most of the first week.

Meanwhile Madonna was doing a few small shows to promote her new album, *Music*, a large-scale tour being out of the question as she had just given birth to Rocco, plus there was the small matter of the December wedding. The London event was at the Brixton Academy on the last Tuesday in November 2000. The stage was decorated with enough bales of hay to fill a barn, which figured heavily in the stand-out performance of 'Don't Tell Me' where Madonna wore that album's signature look, a cowboy hat, and danced what could only be described as a Madonna-flavoured country and western hoedown. It was broadcast live on the internet – I'm not sure the word streaming was used way back then – and when we called Liz in the taxi on the way home to see what she thought of the explosive show, she told us she had trouble watching as it kept breaking up and the picture was fuzzy. Welcome to the future.

The five-song set at the intimate Brixton venue was exclusively from the new album: 'Music', 'What It Feels Like for a Girl', 'Impressive Instant', 'Runaway Lover' and, of course, 'Don't Tell Me'. Short but sweet but oh so sensational. The atmosphere outside the venue was borderline hysteria, with TV crews interviewing those lucky enough to have a ticket on their way in and fans filled with adrenaline-fuelled euphoria on the way out. It was a real event.

Now back on UK shores, Madonna also did a small amount of press, radio and TV to promote the album. She did a short interview with Dominic Mohan for the *Sun* at the Dorchester and, unusually, agreed to have her photo taken by their snapper Dave Hogan (the very same whose foot had been run over so infamously at Heathrow). Madonna was wearing a necklace that said 'Mum' and had asked that it be cropped out of the photo. She looked at the shoot on Dave's computer and picked a shot for the next day's cover. Dom filed his copy, Dave sent the photos to the paper and we retired to the Dorchester bar to celebrate on an incredible high. It had been such a great day. Madonna had been in high spirits and the interview went well. It made both Dominic and myself happy. We couldn't wait to see the paper the next day.

I went to bed on a happy high, oblivious to the nightmare scenario I would wake up to. As I pulled the paper out of my letterbox, I was horrified to see that there on the *Sun* front page was a photo of Madonna *with* the Mum necklace. Before I could catch a breath, my mobile started ringing. Her incredibly irate manager, Caresse Henry (sadly no longer with us), was on the other end and she was not at all happy. Madonna is generally not one to complain about press, despite all the crap that's been thrown her way, but this was an exception.

Of course, it wasn't my fault – some late-night subeditor hadn't carried out Dave's instructions and hadn't used the approved, cropped shot, so I was in the shit. Big time. What made it worse was that we had only just started our own company, not even a month old, and now our biggest client was incensed with me. Not good for the blood pressure. Caresse told me in no uncertain terms that I should keep myself scarce when going to that day's taping for *Top of the Pops*, but rather sensibly I decided not to go. There was no point. Instead I stayed home, eaten by worry that we'd lose Madonna. Indeed, for the next couple of months it felt like I'd been ostracised but Madonna wasn't really in the UK then and when she returned normal service was resumed.

Without doubt, it's the worst I have ever felt during my storied career as a PR. Once you set up the interview, everything that happens is your responsibility. You choose who the artist should talk to and for which publication, and when it goes well, you are a hero. But when it goes belly-up, you are one big villain and you feel awful. It is absolutely soul destroying. To this day just thinking about it fills me with dread. There's something about dealing with the tabloids that only heightens the stakes, and the bigger the artist the bigger the stakes. Back in those heady days, the circulation of the *Sun* was well over three million daily so it was imperative where possible to have them onside.

Madonna did get married at Skibo Castle in Scotland that December and we all started the new year in new surroundings. As soon as Moira and I set up our own business, the phone started ringing with tempting offers to work with new and exciting artists. It was both energising and liberating. No longer restricted to work with what came our way at Warner Brothers, we now had the freedom to choose. And the freedom to decline. As we'd been working in the music business for over twenty years by this point, our contact list was impressive. Although we hadn't worked with other labels, we had connections with many managers and soon they started calling. First out of the block was Trudy Green, who I had worked with as a journalist when she managed the singer-songwriter Stephen Bishop. She now managed Aerosmith and asked if we would do their UK press. There was only one answer.

Another early addition was Depeche Mode. They were looking to change their UK PR, and Andy Fletcher, who I knew through football, suggested me to Daniel Miller, who ran Mute Records, their long-time label. Their new album, *Exciter*, was coming in May. Once again it was a no-brainer, a big yes. Through Andy I also knew Martin Gore, who at the time lived in Maida Vale. I had never met Dave Gahan, their frontman, and when I went to the studio in London to hear some new tracks, I was bowled over by his charisma and presence. There's something about lead singers, about frontmen, that is just captivating. Even when they are not onstage, they command the room.

Depeche Mode work pretty much exclusively with photographer Anton Corbijn on their press photos, album artwork, and often videos and live shows. I knew Anton as he also worked with REM so it felt a bit like family. Now, over twenty years later, five studio albums, various solo projects, remix and live discs, and countless world tours each better than the one before, I'm happy and proud that we still work together. Talk about longevity.

As if the Madonna *Sun* necklace debacle wasn't bad enough, my January trip to LA to shoot an Aerosmith *Q* cover was the absolute worst press trip I have ever been on, one that caused me tremendous angst pretty much from the minute I landed at LAX. As anyone who travels long haul is well aware, your body temperature is all over the place after a long flight, so after clearing passport control, I took my jacket off, got my suitcase and hailed a cab. No sooner was I settled in the back of the cab than I discovered that my passport was no longer in my jacket pocket. It must have fallen out when I took the jacket off. In a panic, I got the driver to swing round the terminal and I ran in, desperately searching for it, asking security, but to no avail. I also went to the airport police station to report it missing but by then I knew that my passport was history.

So there I was in LA with no passport, no photo ID, on my first ever trip where a label I didn't work for were paying for it, with a band I'd never met. It didn't bode well for the rest of the trip and sadly my fears were justified. The passport never turned up so I had to apply for another one. Moira had to FedEx my old passport to me in LA, I had to get Rod Stewart's manager to swear I was me at a lawyer's office and I also had to go to the DVLA to apply for a new passport and then send everything off to San Francisco. The new passport then had to be posted back to me, hopefully before my flight home left LAX. It was beyond stressful but that was *nothing* compared to the Aerosmith shoot.

Q were going through something of a transitional period then and the editor decided to embrace the look of style magazines like *i-D* and *The Face* for this cover. Consequently, they sent two photographers who worked as a team, mostly for style mags, to shoot their first ever *Q* cover. We all stayed at the Mondrian Hotel, though throughout the trip I never met one of them. Apparently, one of them overdid it the first night in LA and ended up in hospital. We were all on the same floor and I walked past his room several times a day where the 'do not disturb' sign hung from the door before eventually learning this story. The snapper that did surface had a plan that involved ten separate locations within the Sunset Marquis. I patiently explained to him that even though it was a ten-page feature, there had to be room for the words, so we didn't need to do so many set-ups.

Prior to my arrival in LA, Aerosmith had sent instructions for their food and drink rider that they wanted on the shoot and also exact specifications on how they wanted the rooms dressed. This was pretty much unheard-of rock-star behaviour for a photo shoot. Sony, their label, was based in NYC and they had no one on the ground in LA who could help so I enlisted one of Madonna's crew to dress the room! The food rider consisted of most of a delicatessen and was more akin to what you'd have backstage for an entire band than a couple of guys on a shoot. Needless to say they didn't use the dressed room – Moroccan themed, if you ask – and the roadies ate most of the deli food.

As I walked to the Sunset Marquis on the day of the shoot, around the corner from the Mondrian, my phone rang. It was Aerosmith's manager Trudy Green, who had shown Steven Tyler the call sheet. She rang to give me the good news that there was *absolutely no way* Steven Tyler was going to do a photo shoot for more than two hours. She actually used the words: 'Would Madonna do this?' And, of course, the answer was yes! Though that made little difference.

When I broke the news to the photographer that we were going to have to work at speed and he wouldn't have as long as he wanted, he broke down and proclaimed that if he couldn't do it his way, he wouldn't do the shoot. That's all I needed. I had no passport, no photographer and pretty soon no Aerosmith. Sony had spent a small fortune on flying us all to LA, putting us up at the Mondrian, hiring the suites in the back garden of the Sunset Marquis for the shoot plus everything else that went with it: make-up artists, stylists – you name it, we had it. I couldn't really tell them we had no cover!

I talked the photographer round and Steven arrived; thankfully he got on well with the photographer and liked his ideas. Guitarist Joe Perry was also happy to do shots in the recording studio that is housed in the hotel basement. The main set-up was in the swimming pool where the snapper had hired (I am not making this up) at least six scantily clad models to swim and jump up around Steven.

Somehow, we got through the shoot. Unfortunately, the photos were practically useless. Back at *Q* headquarters they used the words 'out of focus'. The cover ended up being a casual shot the photographer had taken at the video shoot the day before, a bit less blurry than the others. It went down in history as the worst *Q* cover *ever*.

Thank God my passport arrived the day before I was due to fly home but it was certainly one trip I shall never forget. Luckily things went swimmingly from that point onwards.

A couple of years later Steven and Joe Perry were in London to present an award at the annual BRIT Awards show, on this occasion being held at Earl's Court. For some inexplicable reason, Trudy insisted I go round to Steven's hotel room and talk him through exactly what he could expect when he and Joe did the red carpet. This made little sense as Steven had done numerous red-carpet events throughout Aerosmith's career, but nevertheless I had to go to the hotel and explain that their car would stop, they'd get out of the car, pose for the bank of photographers gathered to do photos, then do a few short sound bites with some press gathered on what is known as a red carpet. It was a totally unnecessary exercise but I was cheered when he greeted me with a chorus of 'My Sharona' as I walked into his suite.

We celebrated our first year of MBC by receiving the Nordoff Robbins Women of the Year Award at a glitzy ceremony at the Intercontinental Hotel off London's Park Lane. Nordoff Robbins is a long-standing music-business charity for underprivileged kids. The award was presented by Elvis Costello, who read tributes from Madonna, Cher and k.d. Lang.

It had been an incredibly successful first year for the company. Our freedom to choose what we worked on paid quick dividends as we took on our first theatrical project, the Pet Shop Boys musical *Closer to Heaven* that Andrew Lloyd Webber's Really Useful Company were producing. Written with Jonathan Harvey, the show opened in May 2001 and ran until October. Reviews were mixed – there's always a lot of prejudice from the critics when artists jump genres. I remember Neil saying he went to bed thinking they'd reinvented the musical only to wake up to the morning papers and read how they'd done anything but! There have been really good revivals since in 2015 and 2019. The score remains one of the best things the Pet Shop Boys have done.

The experience was a tremendous learning curve and it

was a real eye-opener to see how a show is put together. It would not be our last foray into the world of theatre, for a couple of years later producer Phil McIntyre asked us to do the press for a musical based exclusively around Rod Stewart songs aptly titled *Tonight's the Night*. The book was written by Ben Elton and the pair were looking to repeat the success they had with the Queen musical *We Will Rock You*. It was tremendous fun and Rod and Penny Lancaster, not yet Mrs Stewart, attended the premiere.

A couple of years after that we were reunited with the Really Useful Company when we did the press for a revival of *Evita*. That was a stressful, twenty-four-carat gold production, and on the frequent occasions when Andrew's secretary would ring my mobile to say, 'I have Mr Lloyd Webber on the phone for you,' my heart would sink. We were just a little bit out of our comfort zone, but it's good to push yourself. Unlike music reviewers, theatre critics actually have certain seats they prefer for opening night. If you put certain reviewers in the wrong row and not on the aisle, your review is in jeopardy, so we had to learn fast. Luckily all went well and the opening night and entire run was a big hit.

It's really important to know when to say yes and when to say no to a project. Around this time we were asked to take a meeting with Sarah Ferguson, Duchess of York. We met at the Kensington Hilton, which is really closer to Shepherd's Bush, at the end of Holland Park. The hotel was more functional than glamorous and Fergie was businesslike, friendly and instantly likeable.

It was exciting and interesting to meet her. She wanted help with one of her many projects, a charity and perhaps some extracurricular projects. The meeting went well and we were invited to her private residence, Sunninghill Park, near Ascot, where she lived with Prince Andrew. Needless to say we were excited to see the house. It felt like a real adventure. While we sat round the dining room table and had lunch, Prince Andrew wandered in and out, stopping to say hello before disappearing. Tempting as it was, we decided that this was one step beyond and graciously declined the opportunity to work with her.

I'm all for branching out but never want to stray too far from home. It's good to know your strengths and play to them. In 2012 I was asked if I was interested in working with will.i.am, who was about to start the first series of *The Voice*. I had a chat with him over the phone when he was in LA, though he seemed very preoccupied. He was incredibly keen to talk about his charitable foundation and also tech advances in various things he was working on. It didn't feel right so I kindly passed.

The freedom you have with your own company is exhilarating. Every day is different. You never know who might ring or where the day might take you, which is exciting. In the beginning, it felt weird going into Universal Music or Sony or Virgin, as I had only previously been inside the various Warner Brothers buildings as one of the staff. Now I was the outsider, coming in for a meeting, waiting in reception till they called you up. I quickly adapted and soon appreciated how great it was that I didn't have to stay there all day. When the meeting was over, I was gone!

I always tell new MBC staff members that one minute it's January and the next it's Christmas. The days, months and years really whiz by. I'm always looking for people to work with us who are there for the music, not for celebrity. It's really not about press receptions and parties. It's about the music, about working with people you believe in and helping spread their music to a wider audience.

You need to get the balance of your roster right so that you can work with a wide variety of magazines and newspapers, not just one area of the industry. And being independent allows you the freedom to choose who you work with. It's as satisfying getting an unknown some column inches as it is working with a superstar. Perhaps even more satisfying. And as an independent PR you feel even closer and more involved with the artist. As an independent PR, your opinion is just that. They value your opinion, you're an integral part of the team. It's very rewarding.

One sunny spring Saturday I was having lunch in Chelsea before going to a match when the mobile rang. It was REM manager Bertis Downs in something of a panic. Guitarist Peter Buck had just landed at Heathrow from Seattle and had been arrested, charged with drunk and disorderly conduct on board his BA flight, which was totally out of character. Did I know a good lawyer, Bertis asked.

Writing about this now, over twenty years later, it's hard to believe that there was an actual jury trial but indeed there was the following year at Isleworth Crown Court. I vividly remember driving with Peter, Bertis and a few others from the Hyde Park Hotel, out to the courthouse near Heathrow. The scary reality of what might lay ahead filled the car with a massive sense of dread, pervading the atmosphere. I talked about a new Neil Young or Bob Dylan album to try and get Peter to think of something else. It was just incredibly intense. Luckily it had a happy ending and he was cleared, but it was just awful to see someone you care about go through something so terrifying.

Madonna was about to start her Drowned World Tour, her first since the 1993 Girlie Show, and the first time she would be playing indoor shows. The five London nights at Earl's Court in July sold out in minutes and broke all kinds of box-office records. It was fun sitting in the office, announcing one show after another, and added to the tremendous excitement that surrounded the release of *Music*. It was the first time she would be performing the songs on *Ray of Light* too. What a setlist.

The tour opened in Barcelona and by the time I arrived Liz Rosenberg was in a wheelchair, having busted her ankle. We made quite a sight, me wheeling her around the Hotel Arts and into soundcheck at the Palau Sant Jordi concert hall. Liz and I made a habit of digesting the dress-rehearsal shows and making a plan as to what our spin on the show would be, and how best to relay these thoughts to the press. It was important to give them a sense of what they were about to see, to set the tone and hopefully the agenda.

The London shows were literally hot and steamy – no AC in the venue for Madonna – and as good as live music gets. The atmosphere before she went on each night was cranked up to fever pitch as Madonna tunes were blasted into the hall before the lady herself took to the stage.

A few years later, when *Confessions on a Dance Floor* came out, Madonna did a short set at G-A-Y at the Astoria one Saturday night. Chelsea had played that afternoon, and before the midnight show a bunch of us including producer Stuart Price and Pet Shop Boy Chris Lowe went to The Ivy, round the corner from the Astoria, for dinner. By the time we got to the venue, I was flying, and when the Madonna mega-mix blasted out over the venue loudspeaker system, whipping the crowd into a frenzy, I was gone, blinded by excitement.

Throughout the eighties and nineties The Ivy on West Street, just opposite the St Martin's Theatre where Agatha Christie's *The Mousetrap* has been playing since the seventies, was the first real celebrity restaurant in London for my generation. It was strictly A-list and hard to get a table unless you were a frequent customer or incredibly famous.

The white linen tablecloths and lamps on every table were a sophisticated joy as were the waiters in waistcoats and ties. It was wall-to-wall celebrities and industry insiders and it wasn't unusual on any given night for me to know half the place. After my dad passed away, my mother continued to visit London and we always went to the theatre. The Ivy was a must for post-theatre dinners and often the cast of the play you just saw would be dining there. One night during the festive Christmas season we sat next to Albert Finney and Maggie Smith, and my mother had to use all the self-control she could muster not to speak to them. Asking for autographs or speaking to any celebrity you didn't know was strictly forbidden.

Eventually The Ivy became a victim of its own success as other similar restaurants opened, most notably the Wolseley on Piccadilly and Scott's on Mount Street in Mayfair. The Ivy suffered the worst fate of all, opening a chain of Ivy Cafés throughout the UK that to my taste aren't as good as the original.

On the Monday after Madonna's G-A-Y show, I called a few writers who I hadn't seen there. Where were you Saturday night? Did you get in OK? We were there, they replied in unison. We saw you! Oops! Guilty as charged.

Madonna was without doubt the biggest star on the planet at this point and, as she was married to a Brit, Guy Ritchie, practically royalty in the UK. Despite being asked frequently, I always shied away from interviews as I felt strongly that people like me are best staying behind the scenes. However, I did a couple of interviews to promote MBC as we were a new company, and my favourite was an *FT* profile where I was described as 'the closest thing the music industry has to Alastair Campbell', Tony Blair's erudite spokesperson. I think the word formidable was used too. I took it as a huge compliment. More so than the *Independent* profile that called me Madonna's mumsy minder!

By now, the *Big Brother* culture of reality TV had exploded and all the celebrity magazines like *Heat*, *OK!* and *Hello!*, and a lot of men's magazines like *Loaded* and *FHM*, were riding high with massive circulations. A whole new crop of entertainment shows arrived too, including *Pop Idol* and *The X Factor*. It's hard to imagine, but there was a time when no one knew who Simon Cowell was.

The tabloids covered celebrity culture 24/7 too. I always detested the fact that the late fixer Max Clifford was referred to as a PR because he was anything but. He was a celebrity broker and an old-school tattletale who sold kiss-and-tell stories that had nothing whatsoever to do with the art and craft of PR. He was truly despicable. People like Max Clifford gave PR a bad name. It's completely misleading to call him a PR. What we do involves a lot of thought and care. A lot of care and attention goes into deciding which interviews an artist should do and even more importantly which interviews they should not do. Sometimes less is more and it's always crucial to try and only do the right type of press that is suitable for the artist and it's essential whenever possible that both the artist and the journalist feel as comfortable as possible.

There's a lot of prejudice among writers, and taste, like everything else, is personal. Pop music is often dismissed by serious broadsheet writers for no reason. We took on Olly Murs about six years ago. He's someone I really enjoy working with – despite the fact he supports Manchester United. The challenge was to get him taken seriously and appreciated for what he does. The papers are a great platform to change public perceptions. Olly was always highly regarded as being a nice guy but never given enough credit for his pop sensibilities and talent. It was nice to fix that by getting him some quality press that gave him credit for what he had achieved. He was treated like an artist not a pop puppet.

By this point MBC was growing. We took on another office, and then a third even bigger one down the hall, and more staff. We never numbered more than seven as we always wanted to stay small. Boutique was the word we used, and we wisely avoided any of those big-money mergers. Though, truth be told, we weren't asked too many times. We wanted to keep full control and never wanted to grow so big we had to take on artists we weren't so keen on just to pay the bills.

It was lovely to end the year on a high with the Women of the Year Award. k.d. Lang called us 'smart, strong, powerful, kind, funny and masters at their craft'. All true, of course. Cher said we could kick ass as well as any man, and admitted we were the only two women who ever made her shop till she dropped. Of course, Madonna had the last word by simply saying: 'You fuckin' rule.' Who could argue?

A Wainwright sandwich: Loudon, Rufus, BC and
Martha with son Arc, Mountauk, 2012

Chapter 11
Oh What a World

One of the best things about starting MBC was that I was able to work with Keith Richards. Jane Rose was on the phone shortly after our launch, and from that point onwards I looked after Keith in the UK. It added another dimension to our friendship. Ever an astute manager, Jane realised the value of having an independent PR for Keith outside of the Stones circle.

I'd continued to see Keith prior to working with him. There was an unforgettable wedding at Redlands for his daughter Angela in 1998 where Keith, Ronnie Wood and a few other reprobates played an incredible set after dinner and long into the night. It's crazy to think we were all dancing in a tent to this rather amazing live band. His lovingly assembled X-Pensive Winos had even played at the Marquee Club in 1992.

There were more than a few dinners at the celebrity haunt San Lorenzo in Knightsbridge on Beauchamp Place. I have very fond memories of stumbling out of there, full of pasta and red wine, carrying a boxed Christmas panettone down Beauchamp Place, a gift from owners Mara and Lorenzo. Long before The Ivy cultivated its reputation as the restaurant to the stars, San Lorenzo was the place to go. The long line of paparazzi waiting outside its doors was testimony to its pulling power. The food was great – simple Italian – and the atmosphere always buzzing. Eric Clapton and Rod Stewart could often be found there, and quite often Keith whenever he was in town.

Jane and Keith were always incredibly generous with Stones tickets for me whenever they were in London. And I was most welcome to go see the band in Europe and the States. I have the best memories of sitting in many dressing rooms round the world, catching up with Keith and seeing that lovely, warm smile cross his face when I walked in the room. We have known each other a very long time now and it's a relationship that I really cherish. Keith's dressing rooms were much like that very first record-company office I interviewed him in, dressed and draped as if he lived there. A sense of Keith permeates all his spaces, whether home or on the road. Music plays all the time – lots of reggae, Chuck Berry, George Jones, some country, some blues. All authentic. The decor is always scarves draped over lamps. And in the background that Keith cackle, that unmistakable, deep, throaty laugh.

I'd often see Charlie Watts in the corridors backstage and even more often Ron Wood, who always had a dressing room near Keith and often popped in to engage in a bit of banter. Sometimes they were more like a comedy duo than bandmates.

During this period the Stones played a lot of indoor shows, not exclusively stadiums, and I was incredibly privileged to see some amazing shows in small venues, including the Brixton Academy, the Shepherd's Bush Empire and the Astoria. One of my best days ever was another Saturday that began with a few glasses of wine at a pre-game lunch followed by a Chelsea win. One minute I was at Stamford Bridge and the next I was sitting in Keith's Wembley Arena dressing room, a glass of very good red wine in hand, while he and Ronnie ran through a couple of songs on acoustic guitars from my favourite album ever, *Exile on Main Street*, which the Stones were showcasing that night. Life couldn't get much better.

All sorts of artists from my journalistic and/or record label past made welcome returns into my life. I didn't know Robert Plant well during my time at WEA but Led Zeppelin were on Atlantic, as was their label Swansong. When they broke up, Robert pursued a successful solo career and had a UK hit with 'Big Log'. He was often seen around the building, this exotic, golden-haired creature with a larger-than-life personality. In 2002 we started to work together when he released the eclectic, acclaimed collection *Dreamland* and we still work with him now, twenty years later. He once told me that we'd work together as long as he had a career. What I love about Robert and what that statement tells you in buckets is how unaffected he is by the celebrity of it all. What he really cares about is the music, though his beloved football team Wolverhampton Wanderers runs a close second.

Robert is an enormous consumer of music, a real fan. In 2007 he and Alison Krauss made the acclaimed album *Raising Sand*, a country-flavoured disc produced by T Bone Burnett that won Album of the Year at the Grammy Awards the following year. I subsequently sat in many record company meetings where every label tried to work out who to pair various other artists with, to create a winning Robert/Alison-style combination. But those things aren't manufactured or dreamt up in boardrooms. Those things happen when artists truly love what they are doing. Robert even moved to Austin at one point to embrace the scene down there but he missed football and the pub too much so he returned to the UK. In late 2021, Robert and Alison finally got round to releasing the follow up, *Raise the Roof*, to much critical acclaim.

I turned fifty and we threw a big party at Home House, a lively private members' club off Baker Street. Michael Stipe, Mike Mills, Peter Buck and Bertis Downs – in town for Peter's trial – came, as did Suggs, Chrissie Hynde, Andy Fletcher, Neil Tennant, Chris Lowe and lots of friends. It was a celebration of MBC as much as my birthday and my favourite present was a *Sun* front page Dominic Mohan had made up with me on the cover that declared '50 BC'. A strip across the bottom proclaimed: 'Party pictures pages 2–10'. And next to the masthead were pictures of Michel Stipe, Rod Stewart and Madonna captioned: 'Inside – the photos she tried to ban!' That front page still proudly hangs on my office wall.

I was reunited with Phil Collins and Genesis manager Tony Smith to work on a solo album. By now Phil's solo career had eclipsed that of Peter Gabriel and the band. Simply Red embraced MBC, and my old adversary, manager Irving Azoff, resurfaced when he took over management for Charlotte Church and, soon after, Christina Aguilera. It was like the *Crawdaddy* Eagles cover had never happened.

Towards the end of 2002, we were lucky enough to work on the George Harrison tribute concert at the Royal Albert Hall on the first anniversary of his death. Craig Fruin, who we had worked with across several Donald Fagen (of Steely Dan) albums, was overseeing the concert for Olivia Harrison and he hired us. We had crossed paths with George years before while I was still a journalist and Moira worked at Warner Brothers with Derek Taylor, the late, great original Beatles press guru. Another face from the past, Jonathan Clyde, who had run Elektra Records back in the late seventies, was now at Apple and would soon hire us to work with them on the Beatles catalogue, which we have done ever since. The RAH show was one of those truly emotional, magical nights when only music can transport you to another world. Eric Clapton was the musical MD, ably supported by Jeff Lynne, Tom Petty and a star-studded band. Olivia and Dhani Harrison ensured everything was as George would have wanted.

Around the same time, Madonna also graced the Royal Albert Hall for the James Bond *Die Another Day* premiere where she performed the theme. We were sitting in a box with Guy Ritchie's parents – and very nice they were too. The Queen and Prince Philip also attended. The venue was transformed into an ice palace and the party across the road at the Albert Memorial was incredibly star-studded.

Even some of our newer clients were connected to the past. We took on Dido, whose second album *Life for Rent* came out in September 2003. Her manager Peter Leak had managed the 10,000 Maniacs, fronted by Natalie Merchant, and I'd worked with them years before. One memorable night I took the *NME* to see them play a Cambridge May Ball.

Dido was following the insane success of her *No Angel* debut and no expense was spared for the launch of the follow-up as her label, Sony, flew an entire 747 full of media and competition winners to New York. I was in Chicago with REM doing a *Q* cover but had to fly to London, unpack and then fly to New York the next day so I could be on the plane. Talk about jet lag! When I woke up early on the Monday to go to the Virgin Megastore on Oxford Street for Dido's set, I didn't know where I was. After the set, we all headed to Heathrow and flew to the Big Apple. Dido did interviews on the plane. On landing in New York, we checked into our Times Square Hotel – the neon outside my room was so bright I could barely sleep – and hightailed it to the Union Square Virgin Record store for the second live set of what was by now a very long day. Dido stayed in the

US for promo, so on the way home some of us got to fly first class. We were in New York for little over twenty-four hours but it was such fun. The days of spending that kind of money on an album launch are now well and truly over.

We also started to work with Elton John, no stranger to Moira as he'd attended her wedding, as did Rod Stewart and Joan Collins, who at the time was married to Ron Kass who ran Warner Brothers. It was one star-studded affair. Her husband, Clive Banks, had worked with Elton for years. His best man was Bernie Taupin, Elton's long-time lyricist.

We had a meeting at Rocket, Elton's management and publishing company in Brook Green, and were really happy to be able work with him. There was a new album on the horizon and his first ever shows at Caesars Palace in Las Vegas, so 2004 looked exciting.

Just before Christmas, Elvis Costello married Diana Krall (destined to soon be a client) at Elton John's Windsor house. The after-dinner entertainment was a sixties tribute band that literally freaked out when they saw Paul McCartney, Elton John, Elvis Costello and a slew of other celebrities in the room. Eventually some of the guests got onstage for a jam. At some point a Christmas tree caught fire but it was a fantastic wedding.

It must sound like the music business is a very small place and I think actually it is, as those with staying power remain and eventually all work together. It certainly worked that way for me. Many of us obviously shared the same taste in restaurants and shops so it was quite common to run into people you knew and worked with. The Wolseley was the new kid on the block. Situated right on Piccadilly in what was originally a bank, it was quite a space. Neil Tennant and I had dinner there one night and felt like going out afterwards. If we'd been in New York City, we could have gone to the Café Carlyle to see Bobby Short or Elaine Stritch or popped into the bar at the St. Regis for a nightcap. But we were in London, it was just after 10.30 and the best we could do was go to the Piccadilly Tower Records. How I miss those days when record stores existed.

Just as the staff were chasing us to hurry up and leave, Neil picked up a record called *Want One* by Rufus Wainwright and asked if I had heard it. Not only had I not heard it, I didn't even know who the artist was. He insisted on buying it for me. It sat on my shelf till Christmas when I started to play it. The first track, 'Oh What a World', has a chorus that asks: 'Why am I always on a plane or a fast train? / Oh what a world my parents gave me / Always travelling' with the strains of Ravel's *Boléro* interspersed with the tune.

He could write a lyric and a tune. Try this for size: 'a bucket of rhymes I threw up somewhere' from 'I Don't Know What It Is'. Or 'Why'd you have to break all my heart? / Couldn't you have saved a little bit of it' from '14th Street'. Or maybe the best, from 'Vibrate': 'I tried to dance Britney Spears, / I guess I'm getting on in years'. All from this one album, *Want One*. I could go on and on. The list really is endless, and to say it spoke to me would be an enormous understatement.

I devoured the album throughout the holidays and went out and bought its predecessor *Poses* along with his first album and quickly became obsessed, playing the three records non-stop, night and day. Come 1 January I was consumed with a burning desire to work with this artist. As luck would have it, one of the bigwigs at Universal, Max Hole, had worked at WEA in the eighties and I knew him well. He'd been seriously thinking of hiring an independent PR to work on *Want One*, to repromote the record which had come out the previous autumn.

I was in. And once again, my life would never be the same.

BC with Neil Tennant and Rufus Wainwright,
London, 2007

Chapter 12
Somewhere Over the Rainbow

As it happened, Elton and David Furnish had spent most of Christmas listening to Rufus Wainwright too and, like me, knew *Want One* back to front. It gave us much to discuss when we were in Las Vegas for the Red Piano shows, created by Elton and David LaChapelle at the Colosseum, Caesars Palace in Las Vegas which opened in February 2004.

I have travelled a lot, one of the main reasons that Rufus's song 'Oh What a World' resonated so much with me. There is something quite intense about listening to music on noise-reduction headphones on a long flight. It's just you and the artist. It's so intimate. There was also something soothing about Rufus's voice, and for a long time I couldn't sleep on a long-haul flight without plugging into his back catalogue. Of course, the flat bed helped. Not to mention that one glass of wine too many.

I'd never been to Las Vegas so when I arrived – jet-lagged out of my mind because I went via LA to keep my BA miles (insane, I know) – and was told to make a left at Cleopatra's tomb to find the elevator, I was less than enamoured with the place. The minute you land, you hear slot machines and that noise doesn't really stop till you leave. There's nothing in your mini bar. They don't want you spending any time in your room except to sleep, if you must. They want you down there gambling 24/7. Room service? Forget it. It would be quicker to fly back to LA.

The opening of this Red Piano show was a very big deal and I had taken some press over from the UK to review opening night and to interview Elton. He had a new album, *Peachtree Road*, coming out later in the year. One of the writers that came on that first trip was Victoria Newton, who at the time was editor of the *Sun*'s daily showbiz column, Bizarre. That first day, after the long flight, the eight-hour time difference and the slot machines, we went to Spago at Caesars for lunch and a few glasses of wine, and have pretty much been great friends ever since, even though she supports Liverpool. She currently edits the *Sun*, one of the all too few female national newspaper editors in the history of the British press. She's a credit to women everywhere and it's no surprise that Madonna is one of her absolute favourite artists. Strong women attract similar.

I was lucky that many of the people I worked with ended up becoming even more important than when I met them. Many journalists ended up being editors. Countless record company juniors rose from the ranks and ended up as managing directors. The bigger your network of contacts is, the easier the job is.

Piers Morgan, who originally edited that same Bizarre column, went on to edit the *Daily Mirror* and we fell out more than a few times about their often unnecessarily negative Madonna coverage. They once ran an entire page with a border featuring as many unattractive photos of Madonna as they could find and I went nuclear, calling Matthew Wright, who was showbiz editor at the time and had been responsible, to vent. Once they even complained about me in their 3am column. I couldn't really blame them as I always favoured the *Sun* – it sold more and was much the better paper. I have always had a good working relationship with them. The *Sun* and the *Mirror* were the top-selling tabloids, with circulations in the millions, and the competition was fierce. However, I was always a *Sun* reader and therefore inclined to give them exclusives, which the *Mirror* obviously resented.

I saw Piers last summer at the River Café for the first time in years. I really liked him during his *Good Morning Britain* stint. He was his usual acerbic self, very friendly. He asked when I was going to quit working with Madonna and start to do his press. I must say, I couldn't believe the number of women who stopped by his table for a selfie. More than David Beckham and Michael Caine, who were also there that night!

The Elton John Red Piano show was fantastic, a greatest hits spectacle with incredible stage sets designed by top photographer and video creator David LaChapelle. It was a stunning visual spectacle and a total delight. Elton would entertain the press graciously in his sky-high Caesars suite, with incredible views of the sprawling cityscape that stretched way beyond the hotels and casinos. He was almost always funny and charming. Like Robert Plant, he really loves music and follows it obsessively. As an extra bonus, I could also wind him up about his long-time association with Watford Football Club.

In the summer, Boris Johnson came to Vegas to do a piece for *GQ*. He had his daughter in tow for the summer holidays. I only looked after him for his interview and when he went to the show, never, ever imagined for one minute that this rather shambolic journalist would one day become British prime minister. Back in the summer of 2004, he was just a rather entertaining politician with very floppy hair who wrote for *GQ*.

I started out hating Vegas but grew to love it. It's the opposite of everywhere else in America. Usually if you have a glass of wine or two at lunch, they think you're an alcoholic. But in Vegas, it's perfectly normal to walk around with a quart of strawberry daiquiri at 10 a.m., not that I ever did that. A lot of the visitors are verging on the obese as they take the incredibly slow escalator up to the shops at Caesars Palace. Why walk? And don't get me started about the canal at the Venetian. Or the Paris Hotel. It was the closest any of them would ever get to Europe.

One warning: don't go to Vegas in August or even July. The only time you can go in the pool is early morning. By 9 a.m. you are sweating buckets. And if you fancy a dip in the pool when you get back from work, late afternoon, forget it. It's like a sauna. Even warmer. But if you like shopping and eating, it's good fun. And the gambling at low-stakes tables is a laugh. It was a good way to bond with some of the journalists and a great way to people-watch. Some of the characters at the tables look and act like characters in a movie. The wads of cash they carry around need to be seen to be believed.

A couple of years later, the Beatles joined forces with Cirque du Soleil for a rather incredible show called *Love* at the Mirage Hotel, in a theatre that was built exclusively for that show. Each seat had headphones built into the headrest, so you can only imagine how good the sound was. We had a few early meetings in Montreal and visited Cirque HQ to see them developing the sets and songs, which was a fascinating learning experience. Then it was back to Vegas for the preview shows, the opening night with Paul, Ringo and Olivia Harrison, and of course the Beatles' long-time producer, the late, great George Martin and his very talented son Giles, who remixed the tracks especially for *Love*. By now, I was something of an expert on the highs and lows of sin city.

Elton was living in Atlanta at the time, when he wasn't in Vegas or LA, and did a launch show for *Peachtree Road* that November at the Tabernacle to celebrate and preview songs from the new record. I had some press flying in for it and I flew from LA. I watched the 2004 US election results when John Kerry ran against George Bush from my corner suite at the Mondrian Hotel – back at the scene of the Aerosmith debacle. LA is a great place to watch the US election results as you usually know the winner by the time you would normally go to bed, unlike the rest of the country where you have to stay up late into the night.

That October a lot of musicians had taken to the road on the Vote for Change Tour to encourage voter turnout among the young. Bruce Springsteen headlined and REM did a few shows with him along with a slew of superstar, politically motivated bands. On election day, *USA Today* ran a front page that declared: 'Kerry Wins!' But by the time I went to bed, sadly, he had lost. Flying to Atlanta the next day was so depressing. Georgia was a total red state back then and voted heavily for Bush. That would eventually change, when the state miraculously turned blue and booted Trump out in 2020.

Four years after Kerry lost, the Democrats won with Obama getting in. I found myself on another press trip, in Seattle with Pearl Jam, on his inauguration day the following January. It was one of the most joyous days ever as it felt like America was entering a wonderful new era. Eddie Vedder could hardly contain his excitement; Pearl Jam had also played quite a few Vote for Change shows.

We had just started working with Pearl Jam and I had never met them before. I'll never forget my first introduction to Ed. I was awaiting his arrival in the rehearsal studio part of their HQ. The entire warehouse is like a mini Pearl Jam museum, with posters, album sleeves and assorted tour relics scattered throughout the building. Ed arrived a bit bleary-eyed holding a plastic laundry basket full of crumpled clothes he intended to wear for the *Mojo* photo shoot. Most artists have a stylist and a wardrobe rack of just-ironed clothes, but not Ed. It endeared him to me forever, as did the batting cage he had built with a massive collection of Chicago Cubs memorabilia. He really is 'of the people', and when you meet him, it's easy to understand why the band's fans are so dedicated.

That night I took the press out to dinner and the atmosphere in the city centre was contagious. People were dancing in the streets, literally. Afterwards we went to the Tractor Tavern, where X, with vocalist Exene Cervenka, were doing a show, and Eddie jumped onstage and sang with them.

I was reminded of these nights more recently when Biden beat Trump and all hell broke loose at the Capitol in Washington DC. Watching the riots live on CNN, Seattle tragically felt like another lifetime. It was depressing to watch and made me incredibly sad.

My time working with Elton was short-lived. A good friend of his, Gary Farrow, who had previously done his radio promotions, had just left Sony Records and Elton wanted him on board for all his personal media. He was nothing but gracious about it and I completely understood, but it was fun while it lasted. I'll never forget his collection of bobble heads that goes with him around the world and gets set up in his dressing room. He has literally hundreds of bobble-head versions of sports stars, musicians and celebrities – these are always on sale in the States at concerts and sports events. They are called bobble heads, quite simply because their heads bobble. You had to be there. They even have their own flight cases.

Rufus Wainwright's head more than bobbled for a good couple of years before we met when he got caught up in substance overuse. He'd grown up the child of folk royalty: Loudon Wainwright and Kate McGarrigle. His parents separated early and he spent much of his young life on the road. There's a classic photo of a baby Rufus in his mother's guitar case backstage. When I first met Rufus, he was just coming out of his crystal-meth addiction. One of the people who pulled him from the depths was Elton John, who he rang for help when he had hit rock bottom. Much of this is chronicled on his second album, *Poses*, especially the title track when he sings of being 'drunk and wearing flip-flops on Fifth Avenue' which of course you couldn't sing if drunk!

Now hired by Universal to do his press, I could not wait to meet him and found myself one sunny April in New York City at a local Japanese restaurant near his Gramercy Square apartment. I was so obsessed with his music by this point that I half expected the messiah to walk in. He would soon write one of his best-loved songs, 'Gay Messiah', so maybe I was right. When you build someone up in your head, and by this point I thought he was a genius (I was right), they are never quite how you expect them to be. I'm not sure what I thought Rufus would be like. He arrived suffering from a bad bout of food poisoning he'd got the night before at a theatre district Italian staple, and was, for him, low key. Nonetheless, he was probably the campest person I had ever met, and that's saying something. He had an incredible throaty laugh though, as do I, and I could see the sparkle. He was funny and smart, if a bit subdued.

He came to London shortly after as we were re-promoting

Want One, and pretty much from then on he has figured in my life both personally and professionally. The press loved him. His live shows and subsequent album, *Want Two*, were acclaimed. He literally became the talk of the town. Elton described him as 'the best songwriter on the planet'.

On that first promo trip, he supported Sting at London's Royal Albert Hall for two nights. It was a very big deal at this point in his career. He was staying with Sandra Kamen – film composer Michael Kamen's widow – in a sprawling Notting Hill house. That's typical of the Wainwright family. They always know someone, anywhere in the world, and must have a little black book to rival almost anyone. On the morning of the show, Rufus slipped in the shower and fell through the shower door, shattering glass and cutting his hand. He needed ten stitches. He still has the scar to prove it, rather unbelievably in the shape of a W. Not the ideal preparation for such an important step in his career. His manager rang in a panic. Rufus was shaken but like the trouper he is – the saying the show must go on must have been written for the Wainwright clan – he pulled through and delivered a great performance. It was his first at the Royal Albert Hall and the last as a support act. From here on in, he was the headliner. Though he never paid for the shower door.

The UK became Rufus's biggest territory, as they say in the business. And so I found myself in Dublin shooting a cover for *Q* magazine with Rufus and Michael Stipe. I woke up on the morning of 2 July 2005 and turned on my hotel room TV as I packed for my flight home. The BBC news were running a big preview of Live 8, the distant cousin to Live Aid, a massive charity show to be held that day in Hyde Park. Madonna was one of the main artists, and there on the small screen were Madonna and Guy with their kids and my good self, walking them down the red carpet at a London film premiere. When things like that happen, I am always struck by the totally surreal nature of my life. I flew back to London with a spring in my step, knowing it would be an incredible day.

And I wasn't wrong. As I walked into the backstage area, Elton was walking out – he'd been on early afternoon, and greeted me warmly. REM did three big hits, but it was Madonna who stole the show as only she can with tremendous versions of 'Like a Prayer', 'Ray of Light' and 'Music', backed by a massive gospel choir all dressed in white.

Rufus's younger sister, Martha, is also an artist whose golden harmonies surrounded some of his best songs on his early albums. Martha was set to release her debut EP early in 2005 and asked me to work with her. It was titled *Bloody Mother Fucking Asshole*, about her father. This is one family that could never be accused of holding back. Rufus had put the dagger in previously on his classic 'Dinner at Eight' from *Want One*. Obviously, it runs in the family. Her debut album followed the EP, as did an eclectic career that is still thriving.

Rufus was eager for Martha to do well too. However, I wondered if I detected a twinge of jealousy when things did go well. In 2007 Rufus did a couple of nights at Carnegie Hall in New York City, recreating Judy Garland's famous 1961 show there with an orchestra. It was sensational. Stephen Sondheim sat a couple of rows in front of me. I took my mother, who had flown in from Chicago. We had drinks at the interval, near Sondheim, giggling like a bunch of schoolgirls. The Judy show features lots of classic songs, the kind I grew up with. It's timeless and great fun. Martha did a guest spot on 'Stormy Weather' and brought the house down. She did the same in LA at the Hollywood Bowl and the following year in London at the Palladium.

Kate McGarrigle played piano on 'Over the Rainbow' at Carnegie Hall. You can hear her and Rufus comically banter on the live album. It's a hard song to carry off, impossible to better what has gone before, but Rufus nails it every time he sings it. Quite often he would end a London show, sitting on the edge of the stage, and sing it a cappella. It was so emotional, it was hard not to tear up.

When the Judy show hit London, with two consecutive Sundays at the Palladium, Chelsea were playing the cup final in Cardiff as Wembley Stadium was being renovated. I could not miss either the game or the show so did both! Chelsea won a close one, and fuelled by the adrenaline of the game, Andy and Gráinne Fletcher and I had a driver take us back to London. Everything was going according to plan till we hit some traffic outside Reading, where there had been an accident.

On my orders, Moira had bought me a glass of wine, which was sitting by the side of my seat as I finally made it into the Palladium halfway through the first half. Slightly flushed from the journey and still proudly wearing my Chelsea scarf, I was horrified to discover that Ian McKellen was sitting in my aisle seat. Luckily, he hadn't touched my wine, but I had to wait till the interval to sit down.

This really is a story of two weddings and a funeral with this totally unique family. Martha got married in 2007 at the family house in Saint-Sauveur, outside Quebec. The wedding was on a Sunday but festivities began on the Friday night when Rufus played a show in Toronto and Martha interrupted her hen night to come sing a song. The roar of the greasepaint, the smell of the crowd, it fuels the Wainwright family. They seem to be born with that 'show must go on' mentality.

Quite a few guests overdid it that first night but I had

the good sense to go back to the hotel after the show. Jimmy Fallon did not and he was suffering big time when I saw him by the pool the next morning. He'd forgotten his swimming trunks and the only pair the hotel gift shop had were a size too small which made us all laugh when he went for a swim. He'd just been in his first big film and was already a *Saturday Night Live* favourite. Some of the female non-wedding guests were star-struck despite the trunks. Or maybe because of them.

Martha had hired an old yellow school bus to take us all to a lake near Saint-Sauveur for a late-afternoon barbecue and swim. It was idyllic as the sun set and good preparation for the festivities that lay ahead. The wedding itself was on the Sunday. I left my nearby hotel at 4 p.m. and got back at 4 a.m. Now that's what I call a wedding! It was a magnificent family gathering where, throughout the evening, most of the musicians got up to sing on the stage that had been set up in front of all the tables in the tent. Loudon Wainwright opened proceedings, singing a song some would consider in bad taste about the very young Martha. It was as inappropriate as it would have been to sing another one of his songs, 'Rufus Is a Tit Man', at Rufus's wedding. It was embarrassing and I felt bad for Martha. Totally insensitive.

The music continued throughout the night with assorted Wainwrights, McGarrigles, Thompsons (Teddy, Linda, Kami) and Emmylou Harris entertaining us long into the night. Jimmy Fallon even sang a Doors song! There were all sorts of small cabins dotted around the property and one of them was dubbed the drug cabin, for obvious reasons. That must be why I was still standing at 3 a.m., alongside Ed Harcourt, watching Rufus tear through most of his *Release the Stars* album while we heartily sang along in a near empty tent. There were campfires going too that offered a bit of warmth as the night got cold.

Rufus followed his *Want* albums with *Release the Stars*, which Neil Tennant worked on. The album entered the UK charts at number 2 and went gold, selling 150,000 copies. It was some achievement, propelled no doubt by the press. Artists like Rufus, Martha, even Elvis Costello, rely on good press more than other artists who feature in the top 10 and regularly appear on TV and radio. The best artist campaigns rely on as much radio, TV and press as one can get, but certain artists are more radio friendly than others, more press worthy than deemed suitable for television. A lot of singer-songwriters, those whose lyrics tend to make a difference, to really mean something, tend to be favourites of broadsheet rock critics. You have to take what you can get and build on your strengths to create as much noise as possible. As a manager once told me, 'Good reviews don't pay for dinner,' so you need to try to get a good balance across all media to sell the maximum number of records and get maximum exposure. Because press was so integral to quite a few of the artists I work with, the job satisfaction is heightened when you succeed. It was a real achievement to help Rufus Wainwright have a top-five album and it felt great, very rewarding.

While touring Europe, we shot an *Esquire* cover in Lisbon. On a day off between shoot, show and interviews, Rufus took me and Kate, who was accompanying him at the time, on a magical mystery tour of the city by cable car – a must in Lisbon – and we ended up at the toy museum. I don't know many other artists who would take you there! And as weird as it sounds, it was incredible.

Rufus introduced me to opera and I can never thank him enough. His first opera, *Prima Donna*, premiered at the Manchester International Festival, so I worked on the PR for that. He subsequently took me to Glyndebourne, the Metropolitan Opera House in NYC (where I had seen *Tommy* all those years ago), London's Royal Opera House and the War Memorial Opera House in San Francisco. Most opera houses are beautiful, old, handsomely maintained buildings, rich in history. The experience is the other end of the spectrum to popular rock shows. Often there are three acts and you can have dinner, then dessert, in between, and champagne at each interval. It's a lush, relaxing way to see live music and ever so fun. Thanks to Rufus, I became familiar with Wagner, Verdi and a host of others. For one birthday he gave me Wagner's complete *Ring* cycle on CD. Opera, however, is a very expensive habit, so be warned.

One of the most memorable days we shared was when we went to meet the late Stephen Sondheim at his New York City home. I was friends with the people who ran the eclectic modern classical label Nonesuch Records; they knew Sondheim, and amazingly were able to fix a meeting when Rufus expressed interest. We arrived just before 6 p.m. at his townhouse and were asked if we wanted a drink as we were ushered into the beautiful, warm living room. He calls the place 'the house that *Gypsy* built'. Filled with nervous excitement we both said: 'Water.' Suddenly a familiar voice from upstairs bellowed: 'I'm having wine!' Who were we to argue with Stephen Sondheim?

We spent about ninety minutes with him, which went by in a flash. He admitted he never really 'got' opera and it was fascinating to watch Rufus defend its merits. Sondheim was delightful. Smart, engaging, witty, friendly, generous – everything you'd want him to be and more. I had a ticket to see *La Traviata* at the MET that night. By this point, I had developed quite a liking for Verdi, and practically danced the whole way to Columbus Circle, on a total high.

I had arranged the meeting because, by this point, I was managing Rufus. His mother Kate had sadly died of sarcoma, a rare bone cancer, after a relatively short illness. I flew to Montreal for the funeral, which was at the Notre-Dame Basilica where Martha, Rufus, sister Anna McGarrigle and Emmylou Harris sang. It was a fitting tribute for one of Canada's first ladies. There wasn't a dry eye in the church.

I had flown to Montreal with Martha, her now ex-husband Brad, several cousins, a nurse and an oxygen cylinder for their prematurely born baby Archangelo (known as Arc). Several months before, in November, Martha was playing a small launch show in London at the Pigalle in Piccadilly for her Édith Piaf album when her waters broke. Like the troupers that this family are, she finished the set before rushing off to UCL hospital. The baby was born several months premature, and he and his mother lived for quite some time in the hospital. To this day, Martha invites the nurse who took such good care of them to her shows in London.

Emotions were understandably running high in our small section of the plane. Most of the family had been stuck in London in extremely trying conditions for weeks on end, wondering if Arc would be well enough to make the journey, so they let loose on the long flight. The crew were lovely but when several of the party demanded more alcohol just before landing, they were told in no uncertain terms to sit down.

While I was in Canada, Rufus and I had dinner with his partner Jörn, and they asked if I would help them find a new manager for Rufus. After returning to London, I seriously started to think about putting myself forward, which I eventually did. And eventually Rufus agreed. I threw myself 100 per cent into managing him but luckily for us both, less than a year in, he had the good sense to realise it wasn't going to work. He felt it was affecting our friendship. And he was right. It was also affecting my PR company, MBC, as I was spending a lot of time managing Rufus. Moira was very supportive but both she and Jane Rose feared I was jeopardising my career and perhaps my own sanity with this foray into management. And they were right too.

The best thing to come out of it was a series of shows he did at London's Royal Opera House in Covent Garden called *House of Rufus*, a five-night residency – the first for any artist – where he resurrected the Judy show in all its glory for two nights with full orchestra, alongside his own shows with Martha, Loudon and his band. By this time, our relationship was unravelling, so despite the spectacular success of these shows, the whole period was tinged with sadness.

I woke up the morning of the first show, pulled my iPhone from the charger and also pulled my back out. I could hardly walk, the pain was immense and I was understandably feeling very sorry for myself. It was obviously stress-related. Rufus's previous manager got 50 per cent of my small percentage while new prospective managers were closing in. One, from a big US management firm, had even flown in for the first night. Talk about dampening one's spirit!

My back got better but our relationship did not. We had a party at the Ivy Club after the last triumphant night for friends and family. Despite my best intentions, it was hard to celebrate. Six weeks later Rufus and I had dinner in Chicago. I was visiting my mother and he was doing a show at Ravinia, the lovely suburban summer home of the Chicago Symphony where I'd spent much of my youth. We had a very honest conversation, and an incredible steak, and agreed to move forward with no hard feelings. The next night I took my mom to the show and was rather shocked but incredibly touched when he played a new song for the sold-out crowd, simply titled 'Barbara'.

By the following spring we were settling into phase two of our friendship and he invited me to go with him to Westminster Abbey for Commonwealth Day celebrations, where he performed in front of the Queen and Prince Charles. The night before, we went to the soundcheck, among a handful of people in Westminster Abbey. It was spine-tingling. After the-ceremony, we went to a reception at Clarence House, where we met the Queen. As she came past and shook our hands (of course we managed to get to the front of the queue), Rufus told her he had met her cousin, Lord Harewood, who had started the English National Opera. Rufus remembers her saying, 'Yes, he *cared* for music,' before walking on. We were beyond giddy with how the day had unfolded as we walked through Mayfair, off to meet friends at the Ivy Club and regale them with our adventures. It's not every day you meet the Queen.

Rufus and Jorn married in Montauk in August 2012. Like Martha's wedding, it was a beautiful summer day and went on long into the night. Kate was very much there in spirit. I felt more than a little bit odd seeing all the family and friends, no longer managing Rufus, and I suppose my pride took a hit. I had become quite friendly with his immediate family, through various Wainwright family Christmas shows, tributes to Kate and other enchanting musical extravaganzas. I had also got to know his entertaining and diverse network of friends. But like the grown-ups that we are, we continue to work together. Whenever Rufus is in London, we have incredibly fun dinners with Neil Tennant, fuelled by much laughter and just a little bit of bitchy gossip. I always feel sorry for whoever sits next to us on these occasions.

The immediate aftermath of not managing Rufus was a

real low point for me. But it was followed by a real highpoint as the song 'Barbara' appeared on his next album, *Out of the Game*, produced by Mark Ronson. It's a beautiful tune that lovingly references my love of rosé wine. It was an experience I won't forget and now I have a song that will live forever.

Brit Awards, Earl's Court, London, 2007
Left to right: Moira Bellas, Mark Ronson, BC,
Ann Jones (Mark's mum)

Chapter 13
Comedy Central

David Walliams was a Rufus Wainwright fan too, but I didn't know that when we first met at an after-show dinner to celebrate Janet Street-Porter's one-woman show and the publication of her book *All the Rage* in May 2004. I went to the show and the party with Neil Tennant, who was good pals with Janet. And because of Neil, I knew Janet well too. It was a lovely evening. The show was everything you wanted it to be – smart, funny, a little bit outrageous, a little bit emotional. The dinner after was a relatively small affair. Elton John and David Furnish were also there. As luck would have it, I sat next to David Walliams. He was great company. We talked about music, which he is passionate about, and of course *Little Britain*, the whip-smart comedy he and Matt Lucas created.

I was delighted to discover they actually didn't have a publicist and would, perhaps, be open to the idea, especially as the show would soon be moving to BBC1. I left that night determined to work with them. We traded emails and a few days later we were talking to his agent, and then Matt Lucas's agent. We were hired! Our timing was perfect.

Little Britain started life as a BBC Radio 4 show and quickly became a cult favourite. It eventually made a smooth transition to television on BBC3. Created and written by

David and Matt Lucas, it embodied a whole new genre of comedy, an almost documentary style of satirical sketches portraying various slices of life in what was affectionately dubbed 'little Britain'. It was outrageous, refreshing and exceedingly clever. It wasn't the most politically correct show, but good comedy rarely is. Peopled by characters that became household favourites, like Lou who cared for wheelchair bound Andy, Vicky 'Yeah but no but' Pollard, and the only gay in the village, *Little Britain* went nuclear when it moved to BBC1 late in 2004. Close to ten million people were watching the show. It was one of those genuine watercooler moments. The characters were on the front pages of the papers as much as their creators. Their catchphrases became part of the cultural landscape and, for a good few years, it was impossible to avoid.

Within a year there was a live stage show, boxed sets of the radio shows, books of their scripts, a live DVD, Comic Relief, Christmas specials and anything else the BBC could think of. They were so big, so quickly, that Lou and Andy even made an appearance at Live 8. If I hadn't sat next to David at Janet's dinner, I would have never got to visit Portsmouth, where the live *Little Britain* show opened in October 2005.

It's quite amazing to work on something that blows up so quickly; it's a bit like a rollercoaster and you're just happy to be along for the ride. Suddenly every newspaper, magazine, radio and TV talk show wants an interview. It's incredibly exciting. We still work with David, who of course went on to become a bestselling children's author and king of Saturday night TV on *Britain's Got Talent*. I still see him and Janet most years at Neil Tennant's birthday dinners and it's always great to catch up.

Not too long after working with David and Matt on *Little Britain*, we had a call from manager John Noel, who we met when briefly working with the lovely Davina McCall. He had a comedian who was a bit rock 'n' roll, a bit of a rebel, a little bit wild, and he wondered if we'd be interested. His name was Russell Brand. We said yes.

When we started to work with Russell he was best known as the host of *Big Brother's Big Mouth*, the nightly catch-up show with a live audience that followed *Big Brother*, which by now was just massive. Russell had previously worked at MTV but got fired after turning up to work the day after September 11 dressed as Osama bin Laden. He later returned to the music channel.

Russell loved music and one of the first things we did was send him to Europe to review the Rolling Stones and meet Keith Richards for an *Observer Music Monthly* cover. For years the *Observer* had a monthly magazine devoted exclusively to music, an excellent publication and much sought after for PR purposes. Sadly, it's now long gone. Not long after, the *NME* asked him to host their 2006 awards at the Hammersmith Palais. He presented an award to Bob Geldof, who upon accepting called Russell a 'cunt'. To which Russell replied: 'It's no surprise (Geldof) is such an expert on famine. He has, after all, been dining out on "I Don't Like Mondays" for thirty years.' Russell's instant retort to Geldof was a gem. It helped propel him into the stratosphere. Or at least the tabloids.

You can imagine the coverage the next day on radio, TV and in the papers. It was everywhere. Though it was nothing like the kerfuffle (as Lou and Andy would say) a couple of years later when Jonathan Ross guested on Russell's Saturday night Radio 2 show and they prank-called Andrew Sachs, best known as Manuel from *Fawlty Towers*. The *Mail on Sunday* later printed the conversations, which they deemed to have crossed the threshold of what is acceptable and what is not in broadcasting. Suddenly a massive controversy was brewing.

I was having a very nice, boozy lunch at Langan's Brasserie with Chelsea owner Ken Bates and his partner Suzannah when my mobile rang. It was Nik Linnen, now managing Russell with John Noel. As I stepped outside to take the call, I quickly realised that lunch was over. Nik filled me in on events, and within the next twenty-four hours Russell resigned from the BBC and apologised. It made the evening news and of course every front page the following day. The debacle almost started WWIII. Controversy seemed to follow Russell around.

Russell was a man of many talents. He had a very entertaining show on BBC 6 Music before moving to Radio 2. He was as much a writer as a comedian as his many newspaper articles, books, scripts and stand-up shows prove. His stand-up was developing and becoming more and more popular. Comedians often try out new material at small venues while they develop their new show and it's a really fascinating creative process to watch evolve. In April 2006 he started a residency at the Soho Theatre with a new show, much of it about the tabloid media. He'd arrive onstage with that day's papers and literally tear them to shreds. Russell has a razor-sharp wit and is incredibly smart. The words just spill from his brain, out of his mouth, sometimes before he can even digest what he's said. By October he was doing three sold-out nights at London's Shepherd's Bush Empire, much bigger than the comfy Soho Theatre. He would graduate to bigger venues, eventually playing the O2 in 2009.

Russell's altercation with Bob Geldof did not impede his career in the slightest. It only accelerated it. The following year he hosted the BRIT Awards, and later that same year Comic Relief. He landed a role in the *St Trinian's* film and, soon after, Hollywood beckoned and he became something of a movie star. There's nothing like working with people in the early days of their careers, seeing them become bigger and more successful. As artists become more successful globally they spend less time in the UK, less time doing promo and consequently less time with you. It's very rewarding to be involved with an artist throughout their career but there's something very special about being there at the beginning.

We'd never really intended to do PR for comedy artists but it sits so snugly with music that it worked well for us. We met Graham Norton at Matt Lucas's wedding and soon after started to do his press (he and Matt shared an agent at the time). I guess it's what you'd call networking.

We were the new kids on the block and when other managers and agents saw the job we did with *Little Britain* and then Russell Brand, they came calling. What I love about what I do is you never know who is going to call or what is going to happen from one day to another. It is never boring.

One day Tracey MacLeod, a journalist, broadcaster and agent, rang about working with Simon Amstell, who she managed. I knew Tracy through the Wainwrights, as she was good friends with the family. Simon had emerged as an up-and-coming TV personality with an acerbic wit, first on Channel 4's infamous *Popworld*, as co-presenter with Miquita Oliver, and later as host on *Never Mind the Buzzcocks*. His real interest and talent, however, lay in writing and comedy. We worked on the first series of his original, semi-autobiographical BBC dark comedy *Grandma's House* and a series of stand-up shows he did at the time.

When Micky Flanagan's long-time PR went on maternity leave, we were hired to work with him and did so for more than a few tours. We went to meet him and his manager in a pub somewhere in south London, maybe Streatham, which was about as 'out out' (as Micky would say with his most famous catchphrase) as you can get from where I live. He's another comedian who fine-tunes his shows at workshops and we laughed long and hard at many trial runs at the Leicester Square Theatre. More recently I worked with Noel Fielding on his first couple of *Great British Bake Off* series. These days our comedy roster includes Mo Gilligan whose star is definitely rising. It's been really exciting watching him move from online success with his short films to standup in Soho, onto the small screen and now hosting the 2022 BRIT Awards and headlining the O2.

Despite our burgeoning roster of comedians, music remained our main focus at MBC. Elton John's company, Rocket, approached us to work with an unknown singer they managed who had been in the army. He was called James Blunt and his debut album, *Back to Bedlam*, had a song called 'You're Beautiful' that was getting a lot of radio airplay but not much else.

Press is really good at connecting the dots and putting a face to a name, which is exactly what James needed. It seemed obvious that his army background set him apart and, if used correctly, could tip us into the mainstream. Initially the label and management were not keen to use the army angle but I convinced them that was the way to go. They were glad we did when *The Times* ran a big news story on page three of the Saturday paper. It created a buzz and lots of interest, especially with the accompanying photo of James on an army tank, guitar strapped to his back.

The song and James exploded round the world. Once again, much like *Little Britain*, I was working with someone who went from unknown to household name in what felt like seconds. It's a very exciting ride when you are involved from the ground up and it can be intoxicating. That debut album sold over eleven million copies and remains one of the top ten bestselling UK albums of all time.

When this happens, you also travel a lot. You take writers to New York when they play Radio City Music Hall, as James did, or to LA for the Hollywood Bowl. You go from struggling to get coverage to turning down requests and getting more than a few front-page features. It's exciting and you really feel part of the success, part of the team. The more successful an artist is, the more time you spend with them at photo shoots, interviews, trips abroad, after-show drinks, awards dinners. You make friends with their management and the team at their label. It opens up a whole new social life in addition to work.

I won my first *Music Week* award for PR Campaign of the Year for James Blunt in 2005. *Music Week* is the UK's answer to *Billboard*, the US trade magazine, and their yearly awards, especially back then, were extremely coveted.

For his second album, *All Lost Souls*, the label flew key media on a private plane to Ibiza, where James now spent a lot of time when not working, for the launch. James and his band previewed songs from the new album in a picture-book setting overlooking the ocean. For some of us, much debauchery ensued and I recall someone forgetting they had something in their pocket and worrying about customs when the plane landed back in the UK. I didn't have to worry as I had stayed in Ibiza for a few days as Victoria Newton was doing a big interview with James for the *Sun*. After the campaign for the second album was long over, James and the label decided they wanted a change of PR. At the time, James didn't really receive enough credit for either his music or his wit, and was no doubt frustrated with the media perception of him. Years later this would be rectified when he became the king of Twitter with his snappy one-liners and self-deprecating humour.

It's part of the job as an independent PR that you work on a project-by-project basis, and it's always possible that each album is your last with the artist. Luckily we have a very good track record and tend to keep artists once we start working with them. We have worked with both Elvis Costello and Robert Plant for over twenty years, to name but two. MBC is much like Hotel California – you can check out, but you can never leave! And if you do leave, there are different ways to go about this and James took the nice route. His manager Todd Interland and label head Max Lousada took me out to lunch to break the news. And James gave me a thank you gift, an engraved Tiffany letter opener with a lovely note. Not that I used it. I'm very competitive, with a healthy ego, and of course despite the fact that I understood they had a perfect right to move on, I still took it personally. Funnily enough, ten years later, we started to work together again, which just goes to show that leaving on good terms keeps the door open for the future.

We experienced something similar to the James Blunt phenomenon of going from unknown to superstar with Duffy a couple of years later. She was working with Geoff Travis and Jeannette Lee, who we knew from our days at Warners, and they came to us with a magnificent album led by the cracking single 'Mercy' and the haunting 'Warwick Avenue'. Duffy had a voice that soared. We first saw Duffy live at a BBC Maida Vale show at the end of 2007 and the following January she did a residency at the Pigalle Club in Piccadilly. The BBC always have a top-ten poll of the artists most likely to succeed each year. It's bittersweet to look at the poll now: Duffy on top, Adele second. At the time, Adele's career was a slow burn while Duffy took off like a rocket.

I was lucky enough to win the *Music Week* PR Campaign Award for that too in 2009.

We hadn't worked with many producers but as the music business grew, so did interest in the people who made the records. We worked with William Orbit on his *Pieces in a Modern Style* while at Warners and of course when he worked with Madonna on *Ray of Light*. Years later, we got a call about working with an up-and-coming producer so we took the meeting. Expectations were not high when Mark Ronson walked into the office. We vaguely knew his family, as his sister Henrietta had been good friends with Moira's daughter Kelly when they went to Pembridge Hall preparatory school together. We'd see the family at sports days, Christmas concerts and end-of-term events. Mark's dad, Laurence, went to Chelsea and I occasionally bumped into him at games.

I haven't mentioned Kelly before but it's time you met her. She figures greatly in my life and has shared many things with me. I'm her unofficial godmother and she's like a little sister to me. We remain close despite the fact that she is now a wife and mother. As I was always travelling, I was able to indulge her in all the fads from *Power Rangers* to Homer Simpson, *South Park* and of course *Home Alone*, which we both still love. As both her parents worked in the business, it's no surprise she loves music. She's seen some of our artists in concert almost as many times as I have!

The first time she slept over at my house, I had to go and meet Shane MacGowan in the pub opposite Warners first, as the Pogues had signed to the label. He had just come out of hospital and had burnt his hand badly. He could hardly hold his pint or light one of many cigarettes, it was so bad. And being Shane, he was in quite a state. And late. And all I could think about was not wanting to disappoint an excited five-year-old. The dichotomy between the two was striking.

Kelly absolutely loves Madonna and has seen every tour, even the last night of the Madame X Tour before the pandemic struck in 2020. She met Madonna several times, the most memorable of which was in her dressing room at *Top of the Pops* when she spied a Prada shoebox in the corner, prompting Madonna to say: 'I love a girl who knows her Prada.' When I became infatuated with Rufus Wainwright, Kelly asked if she was still my favourite person! She just wanted to make sure nothing had changed.

When Kelly turned eighteen, she had a party at Home House, but it was the same night James Blunt played the Shepherd's Bush Empire – his first big, sold-out London concert – and I couldn't miss it. There were after-show drinks and by the time I arrived at Home House, just before 1 a.m., I was feeling no pain. The first thing I did was buy tequila shots for all her friends!

The next day I woke to one of the worst hangovers imaginable and had to go to Bolton to see Chelsea play what would hopefully be the game that would win them their first Premier League title. I slept the whole way up in the back of a friend's BMW but was able to indulge in the complimentary champagne that was included in our hospitality package by the time we arrived. Rather unusually, Bolton had a hotel at one end of their ground. Our table in the hotel restaurant was behind glass, just behind the goal where the Chelsea fans were. It was a 5.30 kick-off, so by the time the game started I felt practically human again. As I had done most of that season, I bet on Frank Lampard to score the first goal. Not only did he score the first, he scored the second and we won the Premier League for the first time but not the last. It was one of the best days of my life.

Probably the only day that would rival that was when Chelsea won the Champions League in Munich in May

2012. It was the most glorious weekend. I went with Andy Fletcher's family, but without Andy because Depeche Mode were touring at the time. Depeche are especially massive in Germany and their local promoter had arranged transport for us. When Bayern Munich scored in the eighty-second minute, I texted Andy's wife Gráinne to say, see you at the car. But then Didier Drogba scored the equaliser, the game went to extra time and we won on a penalty shoot-out. The German promoters, all avid Bayern Munich fans, took us to a Michelin-starred restaurant after the game despite the late hour. I arrived very happy with a massive Chelsea flag draped over me and the biggest smile on my face. We left around 4 a.m. as the restaurant played Queen's 'We Are the Champions', much to the annoyance of our German hosts. It's a day none of us will ever forget.

Though we worked primarily with singer-songwriters and bands, we were always open to new adventures, like our forays into comedy, theatre and music producers proved. We met Mark Ronson, who was primarily known as a DJ and producer, because he shared the same management as William Orbit.

Mark had put an album out a couple of years before, *Here Comes the Fuzz*, which made some noise, but he felt his career was coming to the point where he needed PR. He'd had much success as a producer with Lily Allen and Amy Winehouse, and was now working on his own album. Both Amy and Lily would feature on that album, *Version*, as Mark uses different vocalists on each track because he doesn't sing. Singing is actually one of the few things he doesn't do!

I liked him straight away; he's incredibly personable and not bad-looking either. He's also quite humble for someone so talented. The first proper single we worked on was a cover of the Smiths' 'Stop Me If You Think You've Heard This One

Before' simply titled 'Stop Me', with unknown Australian singer Daniel Merriweather on vocals. When Mark Ronson does a cover version he reinvents the song and this was no exception. He did the same with the Zutons' track 'Valerie' sung by Amy Winehouse. The album entered the UK charts at number 2 and enjoyed three top 10 singles.

For some reason I thought Mark only played keyboards, and never even realised he was a guitar player till we saw him at his first proper solo London show at the beautiful, retro Bloomsbury Ballroom in May 2007. It was touching seeing his family backstage rather than at those school sports days.

The following year he won a BRIT Award for Best British Male and thanked me and Moira, live on ITV, which was pretty much the nicest thing anyone could possibly do in their acceptance speech. He played a medley of songs from *Version* at the show featuring Adele on 'God Put a Smile on Your Face', 'Stop Me' with Daniel and 'Valerie' with Amy. That same February 2008, Mark won an unprecedented three Grammy Awards. Soon he was on the cover of *GQ*, *Esquire* and the broadsheets. He was honoured frequently at *GQ*'s Men of the Year Awards, *Glamour* Awards, *Q* Awards. The list is endless. I'd always have the pleasure of sitting with him and one of his model girlfriends.

Mark is pretty much the most in-demand producer in all of music but still manages to maintain a successful solo career. During my short-lived stint as Rufus Wainwright's manager, I hooked them up and Mark produced an album for him. In 2014 he blew up the charts with his Bruno Mars collaboration 'Uptown Funk', winning even more Grammys in the process.

One of the worst calls I ever received was from Mark the summer of 2011. I was standing on the side of the stage listening to a Rufus soundcheck at the Royal Opera House when the papers started ringing me to say Amy Winehouse had died. Minutes later Mark rang. All he said was: 'Is it true?' I could barely get the 'yes' out of my mouth before he hung up.

BC and Dave Grohl, Mulholland Drive, LA, 2018

Chapter 14
Band Aid

Bobby Gillespie, Primal Scream main man, came for a meeting one dark January day in 2006. He looked every inch the rock star, wearing a long leather coat and a haggard look that said, 'I haven't been to bed.' The junior came in to ask if he wanted coffee, tea or water. He wanted vodka. Off the junior went to buy a bottle around the corner. An MBC first.

He'd been up all night and, as he now admits, 'was a bit worse for wear'. Nevertheless, we soon started to work together, and did so for over the ten years. By 2008 he was sober and has stayed that way ever since. Bobby and I share a love of the Rolling Stones and all things Keith so it was just a pleasure to work with him. I'd met him a few times with Robert Plant, and of course back in the day with the Jesus and Mary Chain.

Primal Scream had just recorded one of those statement albums that confidently declares its intentions from the first note. They were back on form. The album was called *Riot City Blues* and possessed a real swagger. Produced by Youth, who I had worked with at Warners when he was in a band humbly called Brilliant, the first single, 'Country Girl', tipped a raucous hat to the Rolling Stones and went top 5, as did the album. Two firsts for the band. Happy days. Sadly, it didn't last. *Riot City Blues* was their last album on Sony Records.

Their next disc, *Beautiful Future*, was on B-Unique, a small indie label distributed at the time by Atlantic Records. It wasn't a good mix, not the right home for the band. Five years later they partnered with (Oasis manager) Marcus Russell's independent label Ignition for their *More Light* album, which suited them much better.

I have fond memories of Bobby and his partner in crime, Andrew Innes, excitedly playing me early demos of new material at their ramshackle Primrose Hill Studio. It had so much character but sadly the building eventually fell victim to real estate developers and was sold, then demolished. They upped sticks and moved to a smaller, cramped but still charmingly ramshackle place on Great Windmill Street.

There's nothing better than being in the company of musicians who are still in thrall to what they do. The excitement at the beginning of a project is contagious and it's our job to bottle that feeling and sell it to the media. The first couple of interviews an artist does at the beginning of the project are among the best, as they are fresh and excited about something they have been working on for so long. The difference between those early interviews, when the artist is really eager to get some reaction to their work, and the end of a campaign when they are bored with being asked the same questions is staggering. In the beginning of a project, anything is possible. The score is nil–nil, anyone can win. There are no reviews yet and no advance orders or chart positions to worry about. It's an exciting period and liberating for all concerned.

It's always best, where possible, to vary the kind of interviews an artist does if they are doing more than a couple on any given day. You do not want them getting bored. Once Rod Stewart was doing an interview with *Mojo* and he called me into the room, proclaiming good naturedly: 'They asked me the same question three years ago!' And when doing an interview schedule don't tire them out. Early in my journalistic career, I turned up at a Park Lane hotel excited to meet Steve Marriott, then of Humble Pie. However, the poor guy had been stuck inside the same suite for the better part of a day and by the time I walked in the room he could barely speak.

In between releases Primal Scream continued to thrive onstage. They are an incredibly exciting live band. Bobby Gillespie prowls the stage like a man possessed. In late 2010 they celebrated the twentieth anniversary of their seminal album *Screamadelica* with two out-of-this-world shows at London's Olympia. I'd guess at least half the audience were on pills. People were walking round the venue in a daze, looking for their friends, long after the house lights came back on. Total carnage. But Bobby was straight and in total command of the evening. It was such a success that the band did a UK *Screamadelica* anniversary tour the following spring. Seeing Bobby backstage before the band went on at the Olympia, happy and surrounded by his wife and kids, was just heart-warming. When we stopped working together, he sent me a gorgeous bunch of flowers with a card that said: 'It's Only Rock 'n' Roll.' What a prince.

If it wasn't for Bobby Gillespie, you wouldn't be reading this book. During May 2020 when we were all deep in the throes of lockdown, Bobby texted me to say he'd just read a 1976 interview I'd done with Mick and Keith. The excellent Rock's Backpages site has a lot of my old *Sounds* stories. For years I'd been telling friends, after a few glasses of wine, that I wanted to write a book but the next morning I always got up and went to work. And work is busy. But when the pandemic gave us all a bit more time to think, and with Bobby's encouragement, I spoke with his publisher friend

Lee Brackstone. Not long after, we agreed to work together on this book.

Working with a band is a completely different proposition to working with solo artists. The internal relationships in a band spill out into every aspect of their day-to-day existence. It's a case study in psychology and a fascinating one at that. No two bands are the same. The delicate balance of ego between the frontman and the others is a fragile thing, best captured in that classic film *Almost Famous*. And if you happen to be brothers, like the Kinks' Ray and Dave Davies, or Noel and Liam Gallagher, multiply that by ten.

When you are representing a band, you feel you are there to fight their corner every step of the way. You feel it's your job to defend them, as they are always the underdog in the eyes of the media. As I've mentioned before, the broadsheet papers tend to gravitate to solo artists more than groups. With a band, often the music is more important than the lyrics, and journalists do love a lyric, myself included. But I also really love a great guitar hook.

These days space is at a real premium in newspapers and it's that much more difficult for bands to get coverage. That's why you have to justify their worth each and every time they put out a new album. You need to be passionate. You can't take no for an answer. Every time an obstacle is thrown up, just bat it right back. Take no prisoners.

Just before Christmas 2008, Serge Pizzorno came to see me. We sat in the MBC interview room, the same room Bobby Gillespie and I had sat in. He is the songwriter and guitarist for Kasabian. They were soon to release their third album and were looking for a new publicist. I gave Serge my underdog speech and laid out my case and strategy. I love bands, especially guitar bands. Always have. That must be why I loved the Rolling Stones so much. Why Keith

Richards was for me, the real star. And a good deal of our roster has always revolved around bands. It's such a particular dynamic and you need to love it and understand it to sell it to journalists and editors. You need to understand the dynamics and be sensitive to all members' feelings within the group. It's those dynamics that are often what fuels a good feature.

I lost count of all the times I've covered REM interviews with Michael Stipe and Mike Mills and the writer didn't even look at Mike, let alone ask him a question in over an hour. Beyond rude. But these things happen all the time.

Kasabian were on the threshold of the big time but their press profile had not yet caught up with their live reputation. In the press, they were simply dismissed as football-loving, beer-drinking lads from unfashionable Leicester. Soon after the meeting, I was sent their forthcoming album, *West Ryder Pauper Lunatic Asylum*. (I told you working with bands was a different mentality.) Imagine my surprise when I discovered that the first track on the album was called 'Underdog'. It was a breakthrough album. We got lucky. I'm a great believer in fate, and karma was on our side. The first track that went to radio, 'Vlad the Impaler', had a video which featured Noel Fielding, one half of the outrageous comedy duo the Mighty Boosh. The second single, 'Fire', catapulted Kasabian to the stratosphere. Honours came fast and furiously: *NME* covers, a Mercury Prize shortlist, a 2010 BRIT Award for Best British Group and a *Q* Award for Best Act in the World Today. There was no stopping them.

To really excel as a band, you have to be nothing short of magnificent onstage. And Kasabian were just that. A month after their album came out, they supported Oasis for three nights at Wembley Stadium. Each night Liam Gallagher would squat on the side of the stage, drinking in their explosive set, as if he realised they would soon be the head-liners. Marcus Russell recalls walking into Wembley and thinking Oasis were already onstage, such was the raucous din being made by the ecstatic audience. Kasabian were no longer pretenders. They were the next big thing.

That autumn the band played their own headline tour, this time at Wembley Arena. It was the first time I had to duck to avoid being hit by plastic beakers of beer. At least I hoped it was only beer! Watching from the mixing desk was a dangerous business. They offered me a plastic mac for protection! And they always kept rosé in their dressing room fridge just for me. And to this day, still do.

A couple of years later the band headlined the Isle of Wight Festival. We all stayed outside Southampton at Lime-wood Hotel in the New Forest and took a boat to the site. On the way home, the weather had turned stormy and very wet. An over-served Noel Fielding had to be helped into the boat after the show, so he didn't slip on the dock and fall into the water. Most of the people on the boat were over-served in the nicest, post-show, euphoric way. The band's forthcoming new album, *Velociraptor!* – what is it about album titles with these guys? – was blasting on the stereo system the whole way back to Southampton. As we swayed to the music, no one even noticed how bad the waves were.

One morning in September 2011, I woke up to a slew of emails asking if it was true that REM had broken up. At first I dismissed it, as I assumed there was no way the band would break up without me being given the heads-up. But I was wrong. They kept it a secret and just put out a statement on their website. I was shocked. And sad. Though looking back on the last few years, it made sense.

The bubble started to burst just a little when they released *Around the Sun* in 2004. I remember calling the editor of *Q* and going absolutely mental that the album had only been given three stars in their review. I know reviews are just one person's opinion, and I have to remind artists, managers and labels of this all the time. But when the other reviews started rolling in and they were also three stars, I had to admit that maybe they were right. Maybe it was a three-star album. Sometimes you are so closely involved with a project, love the band so much and have listened to the album so many times, it blurs your thinking. It was the first time the band had received average reviews since I had started working with them on *Out of Time* back in 1991.

Their next album, *Accelerate*, was well received but by the time they were about to release what would be their final album, the prophetically titled *Collapse into Now*, the writing was on the wall. To this day, I don't believe that REM get enough credit for the exceptional catalogue of work they've given us. For some reason time has not been kind to them and they aren't remembered as fondly as they should be.

They rank alongside any of the greats as a fantastic live act. They respected their legacy and didn't cheapen it by quitting then reforming, by doing a series of never-ending farewell tours. They simply broke up. And then they were gone.

Five years later, just before Christmas 2016, they resurfaced with a lovingly reissued package of *Out of Time* and came to London to promote it. We had a reunion dinner at the River Café with their new label Concord, manager Bertis Downs, Michael Stipe and Mike Mills. The following year, we worked on the *Automatic for the People* reissue, and again Mike and Michael came in to do press. By this point Peter Buck was doing his own thing.

In the spring of 2018, my mobile rang and it was Bertis Downs. He sounded a bit nervous. He rang to tell me that the band had decided to change their UK PR and to thank me for everything. As I said earlier, every artist is entitled to change PR. It happens all the time. But after twenty-five years, I had a lump in my throat. It certainly wasn't because we hadn't done a good job, as the coverage for the two reissues was nothing short of spectacular. When the band broke up, they wrote on their website: 'all things must end, and we wanted to do it right, to do it our way'. After I had spoken to Bertis, I waited for Michael Stipe and/or Mike Mills to reach out to me privately. We'd worked together for a quarter of a century, something that rarely happens, so it was not unreasonable to expect a call, a text or an email to say a personal thanks. But it never came. Their silence both surprised and disappointed me. It still hurts.

One thing Bertis did do, before we parted, was introduce me to John Silva. We were working on Savages, a really exciting rock band. They had put out their acclaimed second album *Adore Life* in January 2016 and shortly after fired their manager. By summer they had hired John and he joined Bertis, his family and me for breakfast one summer day at their hotel when they were visiting London.

It was surprising our paths hadn't crossed before, as John manages a who's who of fabulous artists. But for some reason we hadn't worked together. I meet people all the time and thought nothing more of it. By September, Savages had been shortlisted for the Mercury Prize and I sat next to John at the awards dinner. As he is American, I happened to ask him if he liked baseball. I don't even know why I asked him, just one of those random conversational chats, but the answer was a big yes. Turns out he's a massive Boston Red Sox fan and we've pretty much been great friends ever since. He helped get me tickets for the Chicago Cubs play-off games a month later, for which I will forever be in his debt. He knew the higher-ups at Wrigley Field because one of the bands he also managed, the Foo Fighters, had played there.

By January 2017, John had sent me some music and asked me to listen. He wouldn't tell me who the band were until I had digested it all. This is typical of him. I've never met anyone who loves music as much, who respects journalists, writers, who is so knowledgeable and appreciative of the process of what we all do. He drinks in the history of music. The band was Spoon, one of America's finest, and on the cusp of success in the UK. They had delivered an exciting new album, *Hot Thoughts*, which we happily worked on. Soon after that I was flown to LA to meet the Foo Fighters with a view to working with them. They were about to headline Glastonbury, two years after they were originally supposed to, as Dave Grohl had rather inconveniently broken his leg.

Prior to going to LA, John had me write a mini BC bio to show Dave. 'Who doesn't like to write about themselves?' he asked. And he wasn't wrong. I turned up at SAM, John's company, and was asked what deli sandwich I wanted for lunch, as the band were ordering from their studio. How I survived the journey out to the San Fernando Valley I do not know. John has a Mini and drives like a maniac. The Foo Fighters' new single, 'Run', was being released imminently, from their forthcoming *Concrete and Gold* album. In between weaving in and out of traffic on the crazy LA freeways, John was barking into the phone at the RCA head of promo in the US about playlists. In between calls, he kept saying to me, tell Dave about Keith, tell Dave this, tell Dave that, dodging cars as we sped towards the studio.

By the time we got there, I was grateful just to get out of the car! I was ushered upstairs, where the band sat around a big table eating lunch and was given a salt beef sandwich bigger than my head. It was impossible to hold, let alone eat. And there was no way I could talk at the same time. I did the usual BC life story spiel I give artists and managers who ask for some history. By now Dave was sitting on the window ledge, smoking a cigarette out the window. When I got to the part about how in high school none of my friends could roll joints so they gave me their bag of pot and I would always keep some back for myself, Dave laughed so much I thought he'd fall out of the window! To this day I have no idea why that story came spinning out of my mouth.

I figured I'd got the job and I was right. When we were done, I waited downstairs for John and walked around the studio, taking in the history of the Foo Fighters posters and gold discs that adorned the walls. Their HQ is a mini Foo Fighters museum. Drummer Taylor Hawkins talked incessantly about the Stones while guitarist Pat Smear, a lovely man with a gentle spirit, said he had a good feeling about me. That feeling was mutual. I also chatted to guitarist Chris Shiflett and discovered he's a massive Arsenal fan even though he lives in LA. I later took him to a Chelsea v. Arsenal game. Bassist Nate Mendel had left for home. John didn't even say anything about how it went till we were halfway back to LA.

The band were coming over to the UK in a matter of weeks for Glastonbury and I suggested we have a press playback for the forthcoming album a couple of days beforehand. Dave introduced the new album in a studio at Metropolis in Chiswick. It was intimate and personal and a huge success. It really set the tone for the whole campaign.

As for Glastonbury, words cannot really describe their set. The band travelled from London by train and we had a police escort into the site. I watched from the side of the stage. From the first notes of 'Times Like These', Dave had every single person in the palm of his hand. All 100,000 of them. Afterwards, Dave poured a celebratory shot of his beloved Maker's Mark for John, Sony global supremo Rob Stringer and me. He'd just come offstage, dripping with sweat, where he'd done one of the shows of his life. What do you think his toast was? 'To BC's first Foo Fighters gig!' That just shows you the character of the man. The generosity of spirit. People always ask, is Dave Grohl really the nicest man in the business? And, of course, the answer is a resounding yes!

After the show, Dave had to do a quick ten-minute follow-up interview for an *NME* cover that was running the following week. By now he was surrounded by a sea of well-wishers including Johnny Depp and Lars Ulrich of Metallica. I had the unenviable task of prying him away from his friends to do the *NME*. John sat on a couch opposite just laughing and saying: 'Good luck with *that*, BC.' But Dave is the consummate professional and I am nothing if not tenacious (a good combo). The cover, when *NME* was still a print magazine, featured a live-action shot of Dave with the words: 'THEY CAME . . . THEY PLAYED . . . THEY KICKED ARSE'. All true.

When we were driving in the Mini to meet the band, John had repeatedly told me: 'Foo Fighters are the biggest band in the world.' I must admit, I had my doubts. And then I saw them live, and worked with them, and quickly realised how true those words are. I was on a Foo Fighters crash course and went from never seeing their live show to seeing them in Prague, Madrid, Athens, Chicago, Berlin and London within months. Their shows aren't short either. Three hours plus! As Glastonbury was live on BBC TV, there was a massive clock onstage so Dave could see it and hopefully finish in time. He just about managed.

A few years ago, Dave celebrated his fiftieth birthday with a 'Grohl Bowl' party at a local bowling alley in the Valley in LA. Food was catered by the infamous In-N-Out Burger chain, complete with tater tots (way better than fries) and American drive-in style waitresses. Everyone had to bowl, including all the superstar musicians. Grohl Bowl, as it was called, was quite a star-studded event with Josh Homme, Duff McKagen, Tom Morello, Steven Tyler, Rick Astley, Beck and all of the Foo Fighters and their families in attendance.

We were all organised into teams, lanes, times to bowl. It was great fun. And rounded off by an all-star garage-band set from everyone in attendance who could play.

It isn't just Dave who's nice. The whole band is incredibly welcoming. Whenever I go with a journalist to see them, Dave always says, help yourself to anything in the dressing room. Writers can't believe the access. Sometimes artists make writers feel unwelcome. The Foo Fighters invite you in and let you set up home. And of course, this is reflected in the features that are written. Good press is no accident.

And it's not just them. Their crew are great too. Dave's guitar tech even lets me recharge my mobile phone on his sound desk during shows! Everyone who works with them just goes that extra distance. And it pays dividends. When you are miles from the city centre at some festival site, they let you and the writer travel back in their vans. Most bands just don't allow that kind of access. It's pretty much unheard of. And just so you know, they have pizza waiting for them in the vans after every show. And it's hot.

We've had some great times. The best was probably in Argentina when we were doing a British *GQ* cover. Dave woke up the day of the shoot with a massive hangover. And all he could think of was: I feel like shit and we're shooting a cover today! Help! But Dave Grohl is a pro. He took two cans of coke out of the minibar and lay in bed, with the cans over his eyes, hoping to get rid of the puffiness. Genius! The cover, of course, turned out fine.

Queens of the Stone Age were supporting the Foo Fighters on that South American tour as both bands share the same management and are good friends. Their dressing room was opposite the Foos' so you'd have Josh Homme standing in the corridor before going onstage, urging everyone to join him for a shot of Jägermeister. Then Dave insisting the same, except with Maker's Mark, before they went on.

In Buenos Aires, after a rousing set from the Queens, Josh climbed the scaffolding on the side of the stage to get a good view of the Foo Fighters. I was standing on that same side of the stage with a bunch of his Hell's Angels pals. The day before, Josh had gone out for a big motorcycle ride with them. During the second song, Josh decided to throw his now empty beer bottle into the trash can near us from a great height. It didn't make it, and luckily didn't hit any of the band's equipment or us. He sheepishly climbed down and left the stage. A few numbers later, I look up and see this madman, tongue out, sweat pouring from his brow, furiously playing guitar and coming right towards me. Next thing I know Dave Grohl gives me a kiss and then goes back to stage centre, wearing a manic grin. Needless to say, the Hell's Angels were high fiving me for the rest of the night.

The band have friends all over the world and there's always an assortment of them lucky enough to watch from side stage. During one show, Pat Smear saw me behind the barrier and motioned for me to come into the area nearer the stage. 'What you doing with the riff-raff,' he said, laughing, and instructed his roadie to fill my glass up with his onstage tipple – champagne – whenever I wanted.

On another occasion at the London Stadium, I was happily watching from side stage when Stella McCartney, a good friend of Dave's, and her husband Alasdhair Willis arrived. I vaguely knew Stella through Madonna and she'd always been incredibly friendly. They wanted some tequila and within minutes one of the road crew brought out a fifty-year-old bottle and we were toasting the band as they delivered yet another unbelievable three-hour set. I hope heaven is like that.

It's funny to get to work with a band like the Foo Fighters at this point in my career. It feels like I've come full circle. Dave Grohl is equal parts Keith Richards and Mick Jagger. The band tick all the boxes for the fan, the journalist and the PR in me. You always have to remember how it felt standing in line at New York's Metropolitan Opera House hoping for a standby ticket to see the Who. How you felt when you got that ticket. How it felt seeing your byline in print for the first time. How it felt meeting Keith Richards. Or seeing Madonna go from a short set at the Camden Palace to Wembley Stadium.

You have to keep that excitement and wonder in your life. The magic really is in the music. There are hundreds of artists I've worked with that I haven't mentioned here. Working with unknown acts and getting them coverage in the papers is a thrill. I still get excited when we get a new act on the *Guardian* G2 playlist. Or their first big feature. It's what makes the job so much fun.

Not everything is always smooth sailing and I've made mistakes. The biggest one was turning down the chance to work with the then unknown Lana Del Rey. We worked with her manager Ed Millet for years with the wonderfully eccentric Guillemots. He gave me some demos of a new artist he was working with. But I just didn't get it, so I passed on the project, never for a minute thinking she would become the superstar she is today. Obviously, I regret that. But it's liberating to choose who you work with and who you don't. Even today, I'll listen to any new music we're sent. It could be the next big thing. Or even the next small thing but something I love.

Timing in life is everything. Writing this book in the middle of a pandemic, when everything hit the pause button, was ideal. Life stopped and into that gap I jumped head first and took a long look at my life in the pages of this memoir. I fell back in love with my entire record collection. Reading all my old diaries, there are few constants: Chelsea fixtures, Antigua holidays every New Year, visits to Chicago to see my mom, Wimbledon, cricket, lots of travel and lots of live shows. And then everything stopped.

There's no doubt that I'm incredibly lucky to get paid to listen to music for a living. That has to be the best job in the world. I still remember those early freelance cheques from *Rolling Stone* and the *Chicago Sun Times* that said Crosby, Stills, Nash & Young or James Taylor on the pay slip. I thought that was pretty cool. And getting free records, I just couldn't believe my luck. I've never had to look for a job; one thing always led to another.

Moving to London seemed inevitable. When I look back on leaving the US and moving across the ocean at twenty-two years old, it seems mind-blowing. But back then it seemed the most natural thing in the world. Working at *Sounds* led to meeting Keith Richards, and then doing his authorised biography was just an obvious progression. Working at a record company, in what really were the golden days of the music business, was a blessing. Starting my own company – why not? You only live once. I have no idea what's round the corner, but bring it on. I wouldn't want it any other way.

My Phone's On Vibrate for You . . .

I will forever be indebted to my parents, Rose and Sheldon Charone, for letting me grow up in a house filled with music, newspapers and books, and to my sister Jan. I really don't know what I would have done without Moira Bellas, my unofficial editor and everything else in between. Also, a big round of applause for Jane Rose, Neil Tennant and Denise Turner. And a massive thank you to Elvis Costello for taking the time to write such a heartfelt foreword.

The biggest thanks of all goes to the artists, managers and journalists I have worked with through the years and to some I haven't. The magic really is in the music.

Credits

The author and publisher are grateful to the following for permission to reproduce their photographs:

Chalkie Davies (p. 28); Jane Rose (p.48 and p.140); Richard Young (p.124); Universal Music (p. 148); Kat Bawden (p. 166) and Austin Hargrave (p. 180).

Credits